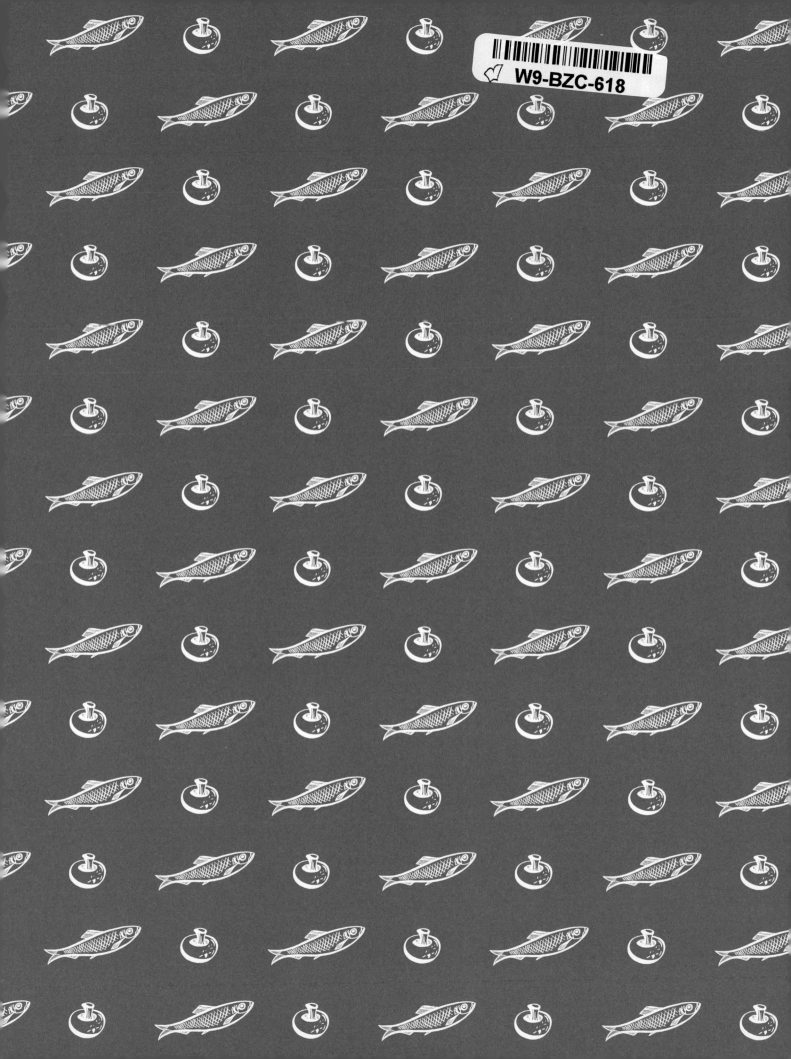

Portuguese

COOKING

Portuguese

COOKING

Hilaire Walden

CHARTWELL
BOOKS, INC.

A QUINTET BOOK

Published by Chartwell Books
A Division of Book Sales, Inc.
PO Box 7100
Edison, New Jersey 08818-7100

This edition produced for sale in the U.S.A., its
territories and dependencies only.

ISBN 0-7858-0187-1

This book was designed and produced by
Quintet Publishing Limited
6 Blundell Street
London N7 9BH

Creative Director: Richard Dewing
Designer: Mark Roberts
Project Editor: Anna Briffa
Editor: Alison Leach
Photographer: Nick Bailey
Home Economist: Sunil Vijayakar

Typeset in Great Britain by
Central Southern Typesetters, Eastbourne
Manufactured in Malaysia by C.H. Colour Scan Sdn. Bhd.
Printed in Singapore by Star Standard Industries Pte. Ltd.

Quintet Publishing plc would like to thank
Peter Wilson for providing the location pictures on
pp 6, 7, 8, 9, 10, 11, 12, 16, 24, 26, 38, 44, 58, 77,
82, 84, 94, 102, 104, 105, 108, 114, 116, 120 and 121.

Contents

Introduction

Portuguese food is robust and generous, designed to sustain hard-working peasants and generate warmth to counteract the harsh winds from the Atlantic and the bitter cold of the mountains. Based on simple ingredients, Portuguese food is essentially unpretentious, with roots firmly based in home cooking and pure, country dishes. Consequently, there are no complicated techniques. Portuguese kitchens are simple with little equipment or utensils. Ovens have only relatively recently become standard in domestic kitchens, so cooking was formerly done on the hob or over a barbecue in the open air. Because it can be difficult with some modern cookers to maintain the steady low temperatures on the hob necessary for the slow-cooking casseroles and stews, such dishes may now be cooked in the oven.

The cuisine has developed from the imaginative use of accessible local raw materials, plus a touch of exoticism derived from the importation of ingredients brought home by the explorers in the fifteenth and sixteenth centuries. Spices such as pepper, cloves, nutmeg, and cinnamon came from the discovery of new routes to the East and access to the lucrative spice trade, while the discovery and colonization of the New World resulted in corn, bell peppers, chilis, potatoes, sweet potatoes, green, and kidney beans, tomatoes, avocados, vanilla, pumpkin, zucchini, and turkey being introduced. In the Algarve and Alentejo in the south, Moorish influences can be detected in the popularity of, for example, almonds and the many sweet cakes and pastries. In Madeira dishes based on couscous indicate links with North Africa.

Not surprisingly, Portuguese cooks make greater use of chilis and spices than most other European countries. While ubiquitous parsley is a very popular herb, lesser known cilantro is also very widely used throughout Portugal.

Portugal runs north–south and is mountainous inland with plains bordering its long coastline. With the consequent variations in terrain, climate and available ingredients, the cooking styles and dishes reflect the regional differences.

Trás-os-Montes, in the extreme northwest of Portugal, bordering Spain (the name means "beyond the mountains") is a region of high barren plateaux and deeply cut valleys, including the Douro. In general, the climate is unfriendly, the land poor and a living hard to come by. Dishes are therefore hearty and sustaining with plenty of soups and stews. However, in the sheltered valleys, vegetables, orange, lemon, grapefruit, and olive trees, and grapevines are planted, but the pigs which roam on the hillsides are the staple of the local cooking. To preserve the meat for the harsh, spartan days of winter, large quantities are turned into sausages and hams; Chaves is famed for the quality of its ham, Bragança for its sausages.

The most northerly coastal region of the Minho has a similar robust style of cooking with, as in other coastal regions, an abundant and good supply of fish. As the land is more friendly and the soil more productive than in Trás-os-Montes, there is a patchwork of fields and vineyards.

Decorated jugs and plates are frequent reminders of the Moorish influence in southern Portugal.

These are owned by peasant smallholders who often grow tall, green *couves* (Portuguese cabbage) beneath trellised vines, to make the famous national soup, *caldo verde*. There are also particularly good, quite firm, full-flavored potatoes.

The three Beira provinces – Alta, Baixa and Litoral (high, low, and coastal respectively) – spread across the center of Portugal. Beira Alta, and Beira Baixa are largely mountainous regions so dishes are of the sturdy peasant variety, while Beira Litoral is a low-lying coastal region, stretching along the Atlantic from Oporto, and the food is lighter with, naturally, fish and shellfish. Some of the best Portuguese cheeses are made in Beira Alta.

Further south is Alentejo, the largest province. On its huge undulating plain, wheat fields abound to produce the main source of wealth for the country. It is therefore hardly surprising that the bread-based soups, *açordas*, originate from here. Cork is the second most important source of livelihood and it is claimed that the pork from the pigs which feed around the cork trees has a special flavor. The plain is also home to flocks of sheep that are kept, not for their meat, but for their wool and milk, which is used for cheese. Rice grows in the lagoons along the coastal side of the province.

Sunny Algarve in the south is the most Moorish part of Portugal (the name comes from the Arabic *el-gharb*, meaning west, as it was the most westerly point on the Iberian peninsula occupied by the

Traditional working boats, moored in shallow water at dawn.

Throughout Portugal, countryfolk take their home-grown produce to local markets to sell.

Ferreirinha are Douro red wines produced by the prestigious Port house of Ferreira.

conquering Moors). The 100-mile coastline was for centuries so cut off from the rest of Portugal in thought and customs that it was known as "the land beyond". The gently rolling coastal plain is known as "the garden of Portugal" as it produces a superb array of vegetables and fruit – tomatoes, beans, onions, bell peppers, bananas, figs, lemons, oranges, tangerines, grapefruit, grapes, pomegranates, apples, pears, and cherries. Almond trees flourish – the nuts are used in marzipan and innumerable sweetmeats. Sugar cane is also grown and rice is cultivated in a patchwork of paddy fields.

Shellfish is wonderful and often inexpensive, and fish dishes are rich and varied; a favorite way of cooking fish is over barbecues on the sandy beaches, either in a clam shell-shaped cooking vessel, *cataplana*, or charcoal-grilled. Sardines, plump and very fresh, are served on slabs of local bread, and accompanied by parsley and sea salt; the juice from the fish drips on to the "plate", which is then eaten.

SPECIAL PORTUGUESE FOODS

Cheeses

The vast majority of cheese-making in Portugal is still relatively small-scale and unsophisticated in comparison with other western European countries. Factory production has only fairly recently begun.

Most Portuguese cheeses are made of sheep's and, to a lesser extent, goat's milk, and on a limited scale by small farmers for their own consumption or for sale locally. The cheeses are seasonal, generally being made during the late winter and spring, and sometimes early summer. Many are fresh cheeses, *queijos frescos*, made into small cakes about 3½ inches in diameter, soft and spreadable. As well as being good with bread, they are sometimes eaten for breakfast, as an appetizer, or sprinkled with sugar and cinnamon and eaten as a dessert.

Some fresh cheeses are left to mature for a month or two, harden and become more strongly flavored. Examples are Tomar, a firm, tangy sheep's milk cheese from a place of the same name 75 miles north of Lisbon, and Rabaçal, made from a blend of goat's and sheep's milk in the province of Coimbra and sold in small straw baskets lined with fig or cabbage leaves. The latter is also often preserved in oil.

Quijo da serra, from northeast Portugal, the most popular Portuguese cheese, is larger and has a fine flavor (the cheese is similar to a good Brie) as it is made from the milk of long-horned sheep that graze on mountain pastures rich with wild herbs, which flavor the milk and therefore the cheese. It is best between December and April.

Evora is a salty cheese made from sheep's milk, occasionally mixed with goat's milk, which is ripened for six to twelve months.

Olive Oil

Portuguese olive oils can be an acquired taste as they are more strongly flavored than most. This is because the olives are left to mature for a few days after harvesting before being pressed.

Portuguese olive oil adds extra flavor to Portuguese dishes but, if the flavor does not appeal to you, substitute an oil you prefer.

Sausages and Ham

Sausages are widely used in Portugal and give a distinctive flavor and character to dishes. Unfortunately not many are exported. In some cases there are Spanish equivalents which can be substituted. For example, Spanish chorizo, which is becoming more widely available now, can be used in place of chouriço, and tocino can be used in place of Portuguese toucinho, smoked bacon. Alternatively, buy a piece of smoked bacon and chop it.

Morcela, a type of black pudding, is used in meat and vegetable dishes. If unavailable, Spanish morcilla can be used instead. Presunto is a quite dark, richly flavored smoked ham. It is both used in cooking and eaten thinly sliced with melon or fresh figs as an appetizer. The best presunto reputedly comes from the Lamego and Chaves regions of Trás-os-Montes, in the north. Westphalian ham is a good substitute.

This wall is actually inside the train station of Porto and is surely one of the most beautiful in the world.

Portuguese ceramic tiles (azueljos) have been famous since the 17th century. This set advertizes a bar in the Algarve.

WINES

There is far more to Portuguese wines than the internationally known brands of sweetish, lightly sparkling rosé wines, such as Mateus Rosé, and light, slightly sparkling *vinho verde*. Portugal has the world's sixth largest area of land devoted to growing wine grapes, and wine production accounts for about 20 per cent of the gross agriculture product. The wines, particularly the red table wines, port, and Madeira are of a high quality and individual style. Wines produced in the top quality 41 defined regions and zones, such as *vinho verde*, and Dão, together with fortified dessert wines from *determinada* regions represent 46 per cent of the total production.

There have been considerable recent developments in all aspects of table wine-making but the Portuguese themselves remain attached to deeply colored wines with high alcoholic content. The basic choice is between the youthful *verde* style and the austere, mature *reservas* (mature quality wines). The most important Portuguese wines are:

Vinhos Verdes

Produced in the Minho area, there are both red and white varieties of vinhos verdes. Best when well-chilled, they make refreshing easy-to-drink summer aperitif wines without food. They can also be drunk with light summer dishes.

Dão

Red Dão wines aged in barrels for several years are deep in color and full-bodied, more in the style of a burgundy than a claret. They go well with game and red meat dishes.

New-style white wines are fresher than the traditional ones, dry, clean and "flinty". They can be good value for money to serve with fish and chicken dishes.

Douro

As well as port, the Douro produces red, white, and rosé table wines. These are pleasant for everyday drinking.

Bucelas

A light, dry white wine for casual drinking.

Bairrada

A vast amount of Bairrada wines is produced. The reds are full-bodied, suitable partners for the region's roast suckling pig, as well as beef and game dishes, and vintage cheeses. There are also good sparkling wines produced by the Champagne method, and much rosé wine.

Alentejo and the Algarve

Wines from these two areas are suitable for casual drinking, especially while holidaying in the locality.

Moscatel de Setúbal

One of the best fortified dessert wines in the world. It is rich, smooth, and honeyed, but not cloyingly sweet.

The winding streets of Alfama, a charming Moorish quarter of Lisbon. It is here that the haunting folk song Fado has its origins.

Relaxing in the sun over a hand of cards.

Port

White – can be either sweet or dry, but is best when bone dry and tangy; it then makes an excellent aperitif.

Ruby – the cheapest port, a blend of wines about two years old; a ruby port may greatly improve if kept in bottle for a few years.

Tawny – a cheap tawny is a blend of white and ruby ports. Good, old, well-made tawny ports are fine, delicate wines and by no means cheap.

Late bottled vintage – is kept for up to five years in barrels but consists entirely of wine of one vintage. It develops a ruby color and a vintage-style character.

Crusted – differ from a vintage in being blends of parcels of two or three different vintages. A crusted port is aged rather longer in casks than a vintage wine, and also spends a prolonged period in bottle, throwing a "crust", or deposit.

Vintage – made solely from grapes of a particularly good year. The wines are matured in casks for two years, then bottled to mature for longer – most need to be kept for between 20 and 40 years to be at their best.

Madeira

Madeiras, from the island of the same name, all have a characteristic "burnt" taste. Madeiras are commonly believed to be sweet, but there is a range of styles from the rich, luscious sweet Malmsey to the light, dry Sercial that is a good aperitif. In between are semi-dry Verdelho and fruity, full-bodied Bual.

CHAPTER ONE

Soups and Appetizers

~

The Portuguese are fond of soups.
The many and varied recipes
generally tend to be hearty
enough to constitute a light meal
if accompanied by good bread.
However, in Portugal they form
only part of the meal.
Except in expensive restaurants,
appetizers are generally
simple and easily prepared,
such as a plate of thinly
sliced presunto
and cubes of fresh sheep's or
goat's cheese, or wedges of
succulent melon.
Aperitifs are often served with
something light to nibble, such as
Fried Almonds (see page 29),
and Portuguese Potato
Chips (see page 16).

Portuguese Gazpacho
Gaspacho alentejana

serves 6

- 1¼ lbs. well-flavored tomatoes, peeled, seeded, and finely chopped
- 1 red bell pepper, cored, seeded, and finely diced
- 1 green bell pepper, cored, seeded, and finely diced
- ½ cucumber, peeled, seeded, and finely diced
- 3 garlic cloves, crushed
- 4 tbsp. white wine vinegar
- 4 tbsp. olive oil
- ½ tsp. finely chopped oregano
- salt and pepper
- 4 slices day-old firm Pâo (see page 113) crusts removed, cubed
- 3–4¼ cups iced water

This is very similar to Spanish gazpacho, but it contains more bread so is more substantial.

method

Put the tomatoes, bell peppers, and cucumber in a soup tureen or large bowl.

Whisk together the garlic, vinegar, oil, oregano, and seasoning; then stir into the tomato mixture with the bread.

Stir in enough iced water to make a thick soup. Chill thoroughly before serving.

Bread Soup with Garlic and Eggs
Açorda à alentejana

serves 4–6

- 1 Spanish onion, quite finely chopped
- 5 garlic cloves, chopped
- 1–2 fresh red chilis, seeded and chopped
- 3–4 tbsp. olive oil
- ½ lb. day–old Pão (see page 113) or other good, firm country bread, crumbled
- 5 cups boiling good chicken stock
- 4–6 eggs, lightly beaten
- handful of chopped cilantro or parsley
- salt and pepper

Açordas are thick, substantial, bread-based soups made from readily available, cheap ingredients. They were intended to sustain peasants during, or after, a hard day's toil. Every scrap of bread, including hard, dry crusts, was saved to make a soup. Beggars used to go around with little bags in the hope of such scraps so they could just add easily obtainable water, oil, and garlic to make a warming dish to fill themselves up. An açorda could be an appetite-blunting appetizer, or, when times were very hard, it could be the main course. Açordas are similar to the "dry soups" of Mexico.
This is the most well-known version of açorda; it is very simple and relies on good chicken stock and good bread.

method

Cook the onion, garlic, and chilis gently in the oil until the onion has softened. Stir in the bread, raise the heat and cook, stirring, until the bread is lightly browned.

Stir in the stock, lower the heat and stir in the eggs, cilantro or parsley, and seasoning. Serve immediately before the soup boils.

Shrimp with Garlic, Oil, and Chili Sauce
Gambas picantes

serves 3–4

- 6 tbsp. olive oil
- 4 garlic cloves, finely crushed
- 2 dried red chilis, seeded and crumbled
- 1 lb. uncooked large shrimp in their shells
- sea salt

The garlic and chilis not only flavor the shrimp, but also the oil. The shrimp give the oil yet more flavor, making a delicious sauce that begs to be mopped up by good bread. Use your fingers to peel the shrimp.

method

Heat the oil in a pan, add the garlic and chilis, and cook for 1–2 minutes. Then add the shrimp and sea salt to taste. Fry briskly, turning the shrimp over constantly, for 2 minutes.

Serve the shrimp in warmed individual bowls, accompanied by good bread to dip into the flavored oil.

Portuguese Potato Chips
Batata fritas

- potatoes
- olive oil
- sea salt

At first I shunned the small bowls of potato chips that frequently accompanied drinks; then I discovered how good they were. There are four reasons for this: they were freshly cooked, good-quality potatoes were used, olive oil was used for frying, and sea salt for sprinkling. Even if you cannot use Portuguese potatoes, do try making your own chips this way.

method

Slice the potatoes very thinly and pat dry.

Heat 3 inches olive oil in a saucepan until it sizzles immediately a cube of bread is dropped in. Add the potato slices in batches so they are not crowded in the pan and fry until just golden brown. Remove with a perforated spoon and drain on paper towels.

Return all the potato slices to the pan and fry again until golden and crisp. Remove and drain as before, sprinkle with sea salt and serve.

Owing to Portugal's long coastline, fishing has always been an important part of the local economy and way of life.

Shrimp with Garlic, Oil, and Chili Sauce

Stuffed Eggs

Ovos recheados

serves 4

- 4 large eggs, hard-cooked
- 8 oz. sardines, canned in tomato sauce
- mayonnaise
- paprika
- lemon juice
- salt and pepper
- chopped parsley, to garnish

Stuffed eggs are a popular appetizer in Portugal. They can also make a snack or light lunch or supper if served with a salad and good bread.

method

Peel the eggs; then cut in half lengthwise. Scoop the egg yolks into a bowl and mash with the sardines. Work in enough mayonnaise to make a light paste. Add paprika, lemon juice, and seasoning to taste.

Divide the sardine mixture between the halved egg whites and sprinkle over chopped parsley.

Green Soup
Caldo verde

The green is provided by couve gallega, *a type of cabbage similar to kale, that has large, deep green leaves. The secret of a good* caldo verde *is to shred the leaves extremely finely. As* caldo verde *is so much a part of everyday life in Portugal, market stalls sell large bags of ready-sliced* couve gallega. *You can also buy a hand-turned machine in Portugal like a giant pencil sharpener to do the job for you. This most basic of soups, despite its simplicity, is delicious and another of those comforting dishes to warm the heart. With good bread it makes a substantial main course in its own right, but in Portugal it is often served as an appetizer. It keeps well and is just as nice, if not better, reheated.*

method

Put the potatoes, garlic, and stock or water into a large saucepan, bring to a boil and simmer for 15 minutes, or until tender.

Meanwhile, remove the stems from the cabbage leaves. Roll the leaves into tubes and then cut across them to shred as thinly as possible.

Mash the potatoes and garlic together in the saucepan to form a fairly smooth pureé. Add the cabbage and sausage, if using, and simmer for about 5 minutes, until warmed through. Season to taste.

Ladle into warmed soup bowls and swirl some olive oil into each portion. Scatter over cilantro leaves, if using, and serve.

serves 4

- 2¼ lb. potatoes, cut into smallish pieces if large
- 2 garlic cloves, coarsely chopped
- 7 cups light chicken stock or water
- 1 lb. spring cabbage or Savoy cabbage
- 8 oz. chouriço sausage, sliced (optional)
- salt and pepper
- 4–6 tbsp. olive oil, to serve
- 1 tbsp. cilantro leaves, to serve (optional)

Sausage and Tomato Soup
Sopa de salsicha

This is characteristically hearty, warming soup from near the town of Chaves, well-known for the quality of its sausages. In the absence of the authentic sausages, use good-quality ones from a reputable delicatessen to be sure of the best results.

method

Cook the bacon gently in a heavy-based saucepan until the fat has been rendered.

Prick the sausages and cook with the bacon for a few minutes, stirring two or three times, before stirring in the onion and garlic. Cook until softened; then add the tomatoes, bay leaf, and stock or water.

Bring to a boil and simmer gently, uncovered, for about 30 minutes.

Remove the sausages and slice, return to the pan, reheat and season. Serve with Pão or firm country bread.

serves 6
- 2 slices bacon, chopped
- 8 oz. garlic-flavored smoked sausage
- 8 oz. morcela sausage or black pudding
- 1 Spanish onion, halved and sliced
- 2 garlic cloves, crushed
- 2¼ lb. well-flavored tomatoes, chopped
- 1 bay leaf
- 4¼ cups vegetable or chicken stock or water
- salt and pepper
- Pão (see page 113) or firm country bread, to serve

Tuna-stuffed Tomatoes
Tomates recheados

The recipe for these tomatoes comes from northwest of Lisbon. I was served one for an appetizer, but two per person plus a green salad and good bread make a light lunch or supper.

method

Preheat the oven to 375°.

Slice the tops from the tomatoes and scoop out the centers. Leave the tomatoes upside down to drain.

Mix together the tuna, onion, garlic, red bell pepper, egg yolk, bread crumbs, parsley, and seasoning.

Whisk the egg white until stiff but not dry; then fold lightly into the tuna mixture.

Place the tomatoes the right way up in a buttered shallow baking dish and spoon in the tuna mixture. Trickle a little olive oil over each tomato and bake for about 15 minutes until tender.

serves 6
- 6 large tomatoes
- 1 x 7 oz. can tuna, drained
- 1 small onion, finely chopped
- ½ garlic clove, very finely chopped
- ½ red bell pepper, cored, seeded, and finely chopped
- 1 egg, separated
- 2 tbsp. fresh bread crumbs
- 1½ tbsp. chopped parsley
- salt and pepper
- olive oil for drizzling

Salt Cod Puffs
Bolinchos de bacalhau

The center cut of salt cod is the most prized, but, being thick, it needs plenty of soaking if it is not to be spoilt by the taste of salt. These puffs are often served with drinks but they can be served with a salad for an appetizer, or a lunch or supper dish.

makes about 35

- 8 oz. dried salt cod, soaked for 24–36 hours in several changes of water
- 12 oz. potatoes in their skins
- 1 onion, finely chopped
- 1 plump garlic clove, chopped
- 2 eggs, separated
- 2½ tbsp. chopped parsley
- pepper
- oil for frying

method

Bring the cod to a boil in plenty of water; then simmer for about 30 minutes until tender. Drain and rinse under cold running water. Remove the skin and bones. Shred the flesh as finely as possible with your fingers and set aside.

Meanwhile, boil the potatoes until tender, and drain. Peel when cool enough to handle and pass through a vegetable mill into a bowl, or mash. Mix the fish, onion, garlic, egg yolks, parsley, and pepper into the potato.

Whisk egg whites until stiff but not firm. Stir a few spoonfuls into fish mixture and fold in remainder gently.

Heat 2 inches oil in a wide shallow pan to about 350°. Drop in large teaspoonfuls of the fish mixture so they are not crowded and fry until an even light brown. Remove with a perforated spoon and drain on paper towels, while frying the remaining mixture. Serve warm.

In many parts of Portugal, life and work remain simple and are still carried on in the traditional ways.

Marinated Fish
Escabeche

serves 6–8 as appetizer
- 6–8 fillets of firm white fish such as porgy, ocean perch, cod or haddock
- 3 tbsp. seasoned flour
- 3 tbsp. olive oil
- 2–3 tbsp. chopped cilantro, to serve

marinade
- large pinch of saffron threads
- 3 tbsp. hot water
- 1 small Spanish onion, thinly sliced
- 2 tbsp. olive oil
- 2 red bell peppers, cored, seeded, and sliced
- ½ tsp. dried red chili flakes
- 1½ tsp. lightly crushed cumin seeds
- 2 tbsp. mild white wine vinegar
- finely grated peel and juice of 1 orange
- pinch of superfine sugar
- salt and pepper

In the days before ready access to refrigeration, game and fish were preserved by steeping them in a vinegar- or wine-based marinade that usually contained herbs and/or spices and seasoning (on the same lines as rollmop herrings). Similar escabeche were also prepared in the Caribbean, as well as Spain. Some recipes are far plainer; this is the most exciting one I have come across.

method
To make the marinade, heat the saffron threads in a heavy-based, dry skillet for 1–2 minutes. Crush the threads and soak in the hot water for 10 minutes.

Cook the onion in the olive oil for 2 minutes; then add the bell peppers, chili flakes and cumin. Fry until the vegetables are soft. Stir in the vinegar and orange peel and juice. Bubble for a few minutes; then add sugar and seasoning to taste.

Toss the fish in the seasoned flour and cook in the 3 tbsp. of oil until just cooked and browned.

Place the fish in a single layer in a shallow, non-metallic dish, pour over the marinade and leave to cool.

Cover and refrigerate for 24 hours, turning the fish two or three times. Return the fish to room temperature 15 minutes before serving. Stir in the cilantro to serve.

Garlic Soup

Açorda de alhos

A very simple recipe using a few inexpensive ingredients to make a filling soup that could either be a meal in itself, or could serve to blunt the appetite before a main course.

method

Crush 4 of the garlic cloves with a pinch of salt, using a pestle and mortar. Mix in the cilantro; then slowly pour in the oil, beating constantly.

Cut the slices of bread in half. Cut the remaining garlic clove in half and rub over the bread; then fry the bread in hot olive oil until crisp and golden.

Put a piece of bread into each of four warmed soup bowls, divide the garlic mixture between them and top with a poached egg. Season and pour on the boiling stock or water.

serves 4

- 5 garlic cloves
- salt and pepper
- 4 tbsp. chopped cilantro
- 4 tbsp. olive oil, plus extra for frying
- 2 thick slices Pão (see page 113), or firm bread
- 4 poached eggs
- 4¼ cups boiling chicken or vegetable stock or water

Garlic and Tomato Soup

Sopa de alho com tomat

Traditionally the ingredients for this soup are worked to a purée using a pestle and mortar, but using a blender is much quicker and there is no loss of quality or character. The garlic can also be added to the blender, but the flavor will be harsher.

method

Mix the tomatoes, bell pepper, bread, and water in a blender to make a thick soup; add more water if necessary.

Crush the garlic to a paste with a pinch of salt.

Heat the paprika gently in the oil in a saucepan for about 1 minute. Stir in the garlic and pour in the soup. Season to taste. Bring to a boil and simmer for 10 minutes, stirring occasionally.

serves 6

- 1½ cups stewed tomatoes
- 1 red bell pepper, cored, seeded, and chopped
- 2 slices firm bread, torn
- about 2 cups water
- 5 garlic cloves
- 1 tsp. paprika
- 2 tbsp. olive oil
- salt and pepper

Clam and Zucchini Soup
Sopa do amêijoas

serves 4

- 1½ lb. baby clams cleaned
- 1 plump garlic clove, finely chopped
- 3 tbsp. olive oil
- 1½ lb. zucchini, thickly sliced
- finely grated peel of 1 small lemon, plus a squeeze of juice
- 1 tbsp. chopped cilantro
- 4¼ cups fish or vegetable stock or water
- salt and pepper

to serve

- 4 thick slices Pão (see page 113) or country bread, toasted
- 1 plump garlic clove, lightly crushed
- olive oil

This soup comes from the Lagoa de Obidos on the Costa de Prata.

method

Put the clams into a large saucepan, cover and heat until the shells open. Reserve the juice and shell half the clams; reserve the other half for garnish.

Fry the garlic in the oil until softened and lightly colored; do not allow it to darken. Stir in the zucchini, lemon peel, and cilantro; then add the stock or water. Bring to a boil, cover and simmer for 10–15 minutes until the zucchini are very tender.

Purée the soup in a blender or food processor, or pass through a food mill. Return to the pan and add the opened clams and reserved juice. Reheat gently without allowing the soup to boil as this would toughen the clams. Add lemon juice and seasoning to taste.

To serve, rub the toasted bread with the garlic and place a slice in each of four warmed soup bowls. Pour over the soup, sprinkle with olive oil and serve.

A beautiful sandy beach, typical of those that line Portugal's southern coastline.

Asparagus in an Almond Coat
Esparagos fritos

If using frozen asparagus, do not thaw before coating and cooking. Mayonnaise is the traditional accompaniment; melted butter and freshly grated Parmesan cheese, or hollandaise sauce, I think make better alternatives.

serves 6
- 2¼ lb. white asparagus (fresh or frozen)
- 1 lemon, sliced thinly
- salt and pepper
- ¾ cup all-purpose flour
- 2 eggs
- 1 tbsp. whipping cream
- 1¾ cups ground almonds
- oil for frying

method

If using fresh asparagus, trim the spears and cut into short lengths. Bring a saucepan of salted water to a boil. Add 3 lemon slices and add the asparagus, except the tips. Simmer for 10–15 minutes, depending on the thickness of the stems, until almost tender, add the tips after about 5 minutes. Drain well and leave on a pad of paper towels to cool and drain further.

Season the flour. Whisk the eggs with the cream. Dip the asparagus in the flour, then the egg mixture and finally the ground almonds.

Heat about 2 inches oil in a shallow saucepan, add the asparagus in batches and fry for about 5 minutes until golden. Drain on paper towels. Serve warm with the remaining lemon slices.

Tuna-stuffed Hard-cooked Eggs
Ovos recheados

Stuffed hard-cooked eggs are a favorite appetizer and this is the Portuguese version I prefer.

serves 2–4
- 4 hard-cooked eggs
- 4 oz. canned tuna fish
- 2½ tbsp. capers
- 1 tbsp. chopped parsley
- 1 tbsp. mayonnaise
- black pepper
- lettuce leaves, to serve

method

Peel the eggs and cut in half lengthwise. Scoop the yolks into a bowl.

Drain the tuna and chop finely with 2 tbsp. of the capers and the parsley. Mix with the mayonnaise and black pepper.

Divide the tuna mixture between the halved egg whites and garnish with the remaining capers. Serve on a small bed of lettuce leaves.

Fried Almonds
Amendoas fritas

Like Portuguese Potato Chips (see page 16), warm freshly fried almonds are a popular accompaniment to drinks. Always be sure to use fresh almonds.

- olive oil for frying
- peeled blanched almonds
- sea salt

method

Heat a thin film of oil in a skillet. Add the almonds and fry over a moderate heat until lightly browned. Transfer the nuts to paper towels to drain; then sprinkle lightly with sea salt.

Asparagus in an Almond Coat

Stone Soup
Sopa de pedra à Ribatejo

The red kidney beans resemble stones in the soup – at least, that is the theory, hence the name. Similar soups are made in other parts of Portugal.

serves 6

- 1 cup red kidney beans, soaked overnight and drained
- 4 oz. piece smoked bacon
- 4 oz. piece chouriço
- 1 Spanish onion, chopped
- 1 garlic clove, crushed
- 1 bay leaf
- 2 carrots, diced
- 3 celery stalks, diced
- 1 lb. potatoes, diced
- 1 cup Savoy or other cabbage, shredded
- 4¼ cups chicken or vegetable stock
- salt and pepper
- ¾ cup chopped cilantro

method

Put the beans into a saucepan, add enough water to cover generously and boil for 10 minutes. Cover and simmer for about 35 minutes or until the beans are almost tender. Drain.

Put the bacon into the saucepan and cook, turning occasionally, until much of the fat has been rendered. Stir in the chouriço, onion, and garlic, and cook, stirring occasionally, until the onion is soft.

Add the beans, bay leaf, vegetables, stock, seasoning, and most of the cilantro. Cover and simmer for about 30 minutes.

Remove the bacon and sausage from the soup. Dice the bacon and slice the sausage. Return to the soup and reheat. Sprinkle with the remaining cilantro and serve.

Crab in a Carriage

Santola no carro

serves 4

- 4 small fresh cooked crabs
- juice of ½ lemon
- ¼ cup finely chopped onion
- 2 tbsp. olive oil
- 1 tsp. crumbled dried thyme
- 2 tbsp. chopped parsley
- about ⅔ cup mayonnaise
- 1–2 tsp. Dijon mustard
- Piri-piri sauce (see page 110)
- salt
- fresh wholewheat bread crumbs

In Portugal spider crabs are more generally used than regular crabs. Spider crabs have beautiful shells and the "carriage" of the title refers to the shell, in which the mixture is traditionally served.

method

Twist off the legs and claws from the crab shells, crack open and remove the meat. Remove the white and brown meat from the shells and discard the gray sac and feathery gills. Flake the meat and mix with the lemon juice.

Preheat the broiler to moderate.

Fry the onion in the oil until softened. Stir in the crab meat, thyme, and parsley and remove from the heat. Stir in the mayonnaise, mustard, Piri-piri sauce, and salt to taste; the consistency should be soft.

Divide the crab mixture between the shells and sprinkle bread crumbs over the top. Place under the broiler until bubbling and golden.

Fava Bean Soup

Sopa de favas à moda do Beira Baixa

serves 4

- 1 lb. shelled fresh or thawed frozen fava beans
- 1 onion, finely chopped
- 2 floury potatoes, diced
- 4¼ cups vegetable, chicken, or veal stock
- 2½ tbsp. chopped cilantro
- 2–4 tbsp. olive oil
- salt and pepper

I use floury varieties of potatoes for this soup as they collapse and thicken it better. If liked, keep some of the beans whole, rather than puréeing them all, to add texture to the soup.

method

Put the fava beans, onion and potatoes into a saucepan, add the stock and bring to a boil. Add half the cilantro, cover and simmer for about 20 minutes or until the beans and potatoes are tender.

Purée the vegetables with some of the cooking liquid and the oil. Pour back into the pan, add the remaining cilantro and the seasoning, and reheat before serving.

Deep-fried Green Beans in Batter
Peixhinos da horta

The exact translation of the title is "garden fish", presumably because the cooked batter-coated beans look like similarly coated small fish. They are usually eaten with the fingers. The recipe comes from near Lisbon.

serves 4

- 1 cup all-purpose flour
- salt and pepper
- 1 egg, separated
- ⅔ cup dry white wine or water
- olive oil for deep frying
- 1 lb. green beans, trimmed

method

Sift the flour into a bowl and stir in the seasoning. Make a well in the center and drop in the egg yolk. Pour the wine or water slowly into the well, stirring in the seasoned flour gradually to make a smooth batter. Leave for 30–60 minutes.

Whisk the egg white until stiff but not dry; then fold lightly and carefully into the batter.

Heat a saucepan or deep-fat fryer half-filled with oil to 350°.

Dip the beans in the batter to coat well and then deep-fry in batches for 3–4 minutes until crisp and golden. Drain on paper towels and serve immediately.

Chicken, Lemon, and Mint Soup
Canja

To make this recipe more relevant for today's cooks, I have used chicken pieces and chicken stock to make the soup, but traditionally it would have been made from an old hen that had ceased to lay. The bird would therefore be tough and require long, gentle poaching to make it tender. It would have been cooked in water but by the end of the cooking time the liquid would be well-flavored and silky-textured. The size of the chicken pieces can be adjusted according to how meaty you wish the soup to be. Lemon and mint give the soup a clean, fresh taste.

serves 4

- 4 chicken pieces
- ½ Spanish onion, finely chopped
- 7 cups chicken stock
- 2 tbsp. short-grain rice
- salt
- 1½ tbsp. lemon juice
- 4 tbsp. finely chopped mint
- Pão (see page 113), to serve

method

Put the chicken pieces into a heavy-based flameproof casserole which they fit comfortably. Add the onion and stock, bring to simmering point and remove the scum from the surface. Lower the heat so the liquid barely moves, cover and cook for 3 minutes. Add the rice and salt, and cook for a further 30 minutes.

Remove the casserole from the heat and leave until the chicken pieces are cool enough to handle. Lift the chicken pieces from the casserole. Discard the skin and remove the meat from the bones. Cut the meat into short strips, return to the casserole, stir in the lemon juice and bring to a boil.

Divide the mint between four warmed soup bowls and ladle in the soup, distributing the chicken flesh and rice evenly.

Deep-fried Green Beans in Batter

Tuna and Potato Salad
Salada atum e batata

serves 3–4
- 12 oz. waxy potatoes
- salt and pepper
- 3 tbsp. olive oil
- 1½ tbsp. white wine vinegar
- ½ small onion, finely chopped
- 4 oz. canned tuna, flaked
- 1 hard-cooked egg, sliced
- 1 small tomato, seeded and chopped
- 1½ tbsp. chopped parsley

to garnish
- sliced tomato
- sliced egg
- parsley sprigs

In the Algarve and Madeira fresh tuna is prized and popular, but elsewhere (and even in those places) canned tuna is used for salads and appetizers such as this well-flavored salad from Sesimbra, a quaint fishing village south of Lisbon.

method

Cook the potatoes in boiling salted water for 10 minutes. Remove from the heat and leave to cool until tender, about 15 minutes. Drain, peel, and slice thinly.

Whisk together the oil, vinegar, and seasoning. Brush a little of this dressing over the bottom of a serving dish. Lay half the potato slices in the dish. Cover with half the onion, tuna, egg, tomato, and parsley. Pour over half the remaining dressing. Repeat with the remaining ingredients.

Cover and leave for at least 1 hour. Serve garnished with tomato, egg, and parsley.

Fish and Red Pepper Soup
Caldo de pescado con pimientos

serves 4
- 12 oz. potatoes, sliced
- 4¼ cups shellfish or fish stock
- 2 red bell peppers, cored, seeded, and coarsely chopped
- 1 large tomato, skinned, seeded, and chopped
- 2 garlic cloves
- pinch of toasted and ground cumin seeds
- 1 tsp. paprika
- 3 tbsp. olive oil
- 9 oz. firm white fish such as hake or halibut, cut into chunks
- salt and pepper
- chopped cilantro, to garnish

Sieved potatoes provide the thickening for this pink-tinged, lightly spiced soup. The fish is varied according to what is the best of the catch that is available at the time; I like to add a few jumbo shrimp, each cut into two or three pieces.

method

Cook the potatoes in the stock until tender. Meanwhile, purée the bell peppers, tomato, garlic, cumin, paprika, and oil in a blender.

Remove about a third of the potatoes and reserve. Add the fish to the remaining potatoes and cook gently for about 3 minutes until the fish is almost cooked.

Press the reserved potatoes through a sieve into a bowl. Stir in the puréed mixture and stir gently into the pan. Heat through and adjust the seasoning. Serve garnished with cilantro.

Tuna and Potato Salad

CHAPTER TWO

Fish and Shellfish

~

As Portugal has a long coastline, and many freshwater rivers and streams, it is not surprising that there is both an abundance and a variety of fish and shellfish including hake, halibut, trout, sardines, tuna, crabs, and shrimp. The big anomaly is cod, which the Portuguese prefer salted and dried as the ubiquitous bacalhau *rather than fresh (reputedly there are 365 different versions of* bacalhau *dishes).*

Grilled Sardines
Sardinhas assadas

Sardines are an essential part of Portuguese summertime eating when the fish are cheap, and at their sweetest and most succulent. Not only are they cooked on barbecues but they can be bought from small outdoor charcoal grills on many of the beaches, and in Lisbon, especially on 13 June when sardines are eaten to celebrate the eve of St Anthony's festival.

serves 4
- 16–24 sardines depending on size
- sea salt
- olive oil

method
Rinse the sardines and remove the scales. Sprinkle the fish with sea salt and leave for 1 hour.

Preheat the barbecue or broiler.

Rinse the sardines and pat dry with paper towels. Brush with oil and grill or broil for about 3 minutes on each side depending on size.

Hake Baked with Potatoes
Pescada à moda do Minho

The Portuguese are great enthusiasts for, and experts on, cooking this fish which is similar to the cod family. This is one of the most delicious of their many hake recipes because by the end of the cooking the fish is moist, well-flavored and succulent, with the soft and sweet onions browning appetizingly around the edges. The potatoes which surround the fish absorb all the mingled flavors.

serves 4
- olive oil
- 1¼ lb. Spanish onions, sliced thinly
- salt and pepper
- 2¼ lb. waxy potatoes
- 8 plump garlic cloves, unpeeled
- several sprigs of chopped parsley
- 4 thick hake steaks

method
Heat 2 tbsp. oil in a heavy-based skillet. Add the onions, sprinkle with salt and cook gently, stirring occasionally, until softened, reduced, and golden brown.

Preheat the oven to 400°.

Cook the potatoes in boiling, salted water until tender, adding the garlic about 4 minutes before the potatoes are ready. Cut the potatoes into thickish slices and peel and slice the garlic.

Lay a thick layer of potatoes in the bottom of an oiled, shallow baking dish so that the fish will just fit in a single layer; add some of the garlic slices to the potatoes.

Spread over one-third of the onions and sprinkle with pepper and some of the parsley. Place the fish steaks on top, season and scatter over the remaining parsley. Tuck the remaining potatoes and some more garlic down the sides of the dish. Spread the remaining onion over the fish, season with more pepper and scatter with the remaining garlic. Trickle over a little olive oil and bake for 25–30 minutes until the fish is just cooked; check to ensure that it does not become overcooked.

Grilled Sardines

Salt Cod with Onions and Potatoes

Bacalhau à Gomes de Sá

This dish, one of the most famous salt cod dishes, comes from Porto, and is named after a restaurateur, Gomes de Sá, who is reputed to have been its creator.

serves 4

- 1 lb. salt cod, well-soaked
- 1½ lb. even-sized potatoes, unpeeled
- 1 Spanish onion, sliced thinly into rings
- 3 tbsp. olive oil
- 16 oil-cured olives, pitted
- leaves from a large bunch of chopped parsley (about 1 oz.)
- pepper
- 2 hard-cooked eggs, peeled and quartered
- chopped parsley and pitted black olives, to garnish
- lemon wedges, to serve

method

Put the cod into a saucepan, cover with water and simmer for 15 minutes. Drain and leave until cool. Remove and discard any skin and bones. Flake the flesh.

Boil the potatoes until tender. Drain and leave until cool enough to handle; then peel and slice thinly.

Meanwhile, cook the onion in the oil until softened. Preheat the oven to 350°.

Layer the potatoes, onion and fish in a well-oiled baking dish, sprinkling each layer with pitted olives, parsley, and pepper. Finish with a layer of onion rings. Bake for 35–40 minutes until lightly browned.

Arrange the quartered eggs on top and garnish with parsley and black olives. Serve with lemon wedges.

Salt Cod and Potato Pie
Bacalhau à Gomes de Sá

serves 4–6

- 2¼ lb. dried salt cod, cut into several pieces, well-soaked
- ¼ cup butter, plus extra for dotting
- 3 tbsp. finely chopped onion
- 2 garlic cloves, crushed
- 6 tbsp. all-purpose flour
- 1¼ cups milk
- 4 tbsp. finely chopped parsley
- 2 tbsp. olive oil
- 1¾ lb. waxy potatoes, parboiled and sliced
- pepper
- 3 hard-cooked eggs, peeled and sliced, to garnish
- handful of pitted black olives, to garnish

This is another version of the recipe on page 42. It is more sophisticated and time-consuming to prepare, but it is moister and has a less pronounced taste of salt cod.

method

Put the cod into a large saucepan and cover with fresh water. Bring to simmering point and then cook gently for 10 minutes without allowing the water to boil. Remove the saucepan from the heat and leave for 15 minutes; then drain, reserving ⅔ cup of the liquid. Skin, bone, and flake the fish.

Preheat the oven to 400°F.

Melt the butter, add the onion and garlic and cook until softened. Stir in the flour and cook for 1 minute; then pour in the milk slowly, stirring. Add the reserved cooking liquid and bring to a boil, stirring. Simmer for a few minutes. Add half the parsley.

Heat the oil, add the potatoes and fry until brown. Line a large baking dish with half the potatoes and combine the rest with the fish and parsley sauce. Season with plenty of pepper and spoon into the dish. Dot with butter and bake for about 20 minutes until golden.

Garnish with the remaining parsley, the eggs, and olives.

Cork tree, Evora. In the granary province of Alentejo, cork is the second most important source of wealth.

Baked Fish with Tomatoes
Pargo assada Lisboeta

Pargo *translates as "sea bream" and is the member of the bream family. Use porgy or ocean perch in this recipe.*

method
Preheat the oven to 350°.

Pour the oil into a shallow baking dish large enough to hold the fish. Scatter over half the tomatoes, onion, garlic, and cilantro. Lay the fish on top, season and cover with the remaining tomatoes, onion, garlic, and cilantro. Pour the wine into the dish but not over the fish. Bake for 35–45 minutes, basting the fish frequently.

Transfer the fish to a warmed serving plate and keep warm in the oven with the heat turned off and the door propped open. If necessary, pour the sauce from the dish into a saucepan and boil to thicken. Pour over the fish and garnish with cilantro sprigs.

serves 4–6
- 2 tbsp. olive oil
- 6 tomatoes, skinned, seeded, and chopped
- 1 small onion, finely chopped
- 1 small garlic clove, finely chopped
- 1½ tbsp. chopped cilantro
- 3½ lb. porgy, cleaned
- salt and pepper
- ⅔ cup medium-bodied dry white wine
- sprigs of cilantro, to garnish

Fish with Parsley Sauce
Linguado com salsa verde

Here the ubiquitous potato is used as the base for a very simple way to make parsley sauce for serving with fish.

method
Chop the garlic and parsley together.

Boil the potato until tender, then drain, reserving some of the cooking liquid. When the potato is cool enough to handle, peel it and mash with the garlic, parsley, wine vinegar, oil, and seasoning, adding a little of the reserved potato water if necessary to loosen the mixture. Spoon into a small bowl.

Season the fish fillets. Heat the wine and stock in a wide shallow pan, add the fish in a single layer and poach gently for about 8 minutes, depending on the thickness of the fillets, until the flesh flakes when tested with the point of a knife.

Transfer the fish to warmed plates and serve with the parsley sauce.

serves 4
- 1 small garlic clove
- bunch of parsley
- 1 small potato, unpeeled
- 1 tbsp. wine vinegar
- 2 tbsp. olive oil
- salt and pepper
- 8 flounder fillets
- 4 tbsp. medium-bodied dry white wine
- 4 tbsp. fish stock

Trout in Tomato Sauce
Truta com tomatada

serves 4
- 1 oz. parsley
- 1 garlic clove, chopped
- 3 tbsp. olive oil
- 1¼ lb. well-flavored tomatoes, skinned, seeded, and chopped
- ½ tsp. tomato paste
- salt and pepper
- 4 trout, about 7 oz.

Wonderfully fresh and tender young trout are to be found in the Serra da Estrela. Choose smallish trout that do not have thick skins.

method

Fry the parsley and garlic in the oil in a pan large enough to hold the fish in a single layer, for 1–2 minutes. Stir in the tomatoes and tomato paste and simmer for 5 minutes.

Season the sauce, add the trout and spoon some of the sauce over them to half-cover. Cover and cook gently for about 20 minutes.

Baked Sardines
Sardinhas à Setúbal

serves 4
- 2¼ lb. fresh sardines, scaled, gutted, and heads removed
- salt and pepper
- 1 tbsp. olive oil
- 1¼ cups tomatoes, skinned, seeded, and diced
- 1 garlic clove, finely chopped
- 1 small onion, finely chopped
- leaves from a bunch of both parsley and dill, chopped
- scant 1 cup dry white wine

When it is not convenient to cook sardines over charcoal, or simply for a change, the fish are often baked with tomatoes and herbs.

method

Preheat the oven to 350°.

Season the fish and brush with half the oil. Use the remaining oil to grease a shallow baking dish.

Mix together the tomatoes, garlic, onion, herbs, wine, and seasoning, and spread over the bottom of the dish. Put the sardines on top, pushing them into the tomato mixture. Bake for 5–6 minutes.

Clams with Garlic Sausage, Ham, and Cilantro
Ameîjoas na cataplana

This spicy, fragrant clam dish comes from the Algarve, where it is cooked in a cataplana, a clam-shaped pan traditionally made of copper but now also of aluminum (see page 56-7). The lid, which is hinged at the back like a clam shell, is clamped firmly in place by clasps on either side, so the pan can be turned over during cooking with no danger of the contents leaking out. However, the recipe can be cooked successfully in a saucepan or flameproof casserole with a very tight-fitting lid.

method

Heat the oil in a saucepan or flameproof casserole. Add the onions and garlic and cook, stirring occasionally, until softened but not colored.

Stir the sausage, ham, and Piri-piri sauce or hot pepper sauce into the onions. Cover and cook fairly gently, shaking the pan occasionally, for 15 minutes.

Meanwhile, scrub the clams clean and rinse them thoroughly under cold running water.

Add the clams, cilantro and salt to taste to the mixture in the pan. Cover and cook for a further 5–6 minutes, shaking the pan occasionally, until the clams open. Serve from the pan.

serves 4
- 2 tbsp. olive oil
- 2 onions, chopped
- 1–2 garlic cloves, finely chopped
- 3 oz. chouriço, or other garlic-flavored smoked sausage
- 3 oz. smoked ham, chopped
- about 1 tsp. Piri-piri sauce (see page 110), or hot pepper sauce, to taste
- 2¼ lb. clams
- 1½ tbsp. chopped cilantro
- salt

Fish Fillets with Tomato Sauce
Filetes à Portuguesa

Fillets of white fish, such as whiting and sole or flounder, are particularly popular in the Arrábida area and in Lisbon. A favorite Portuguese way of serving them is accompanied by a tomato sauce.

serves 4

- 5 tbsp. butter
- 1 onion, finely chopped
- 1 garlic clove, crushed
- 1¼ lb. tomatoes, skinned, seeded, and chopped
- ½ cup fish stock
- ½ cup dry white wine
- 1 tbsp. chopped parsley
- 1½ lb. white fish fillets
- salt and pepper

method

Melt 2 tbsp. of the butter in a saucepan and cook the onion and garlic until softened. Add the tomatoes, half the stock and half the wine, and the parsley. Simmer, stirring occasionally, until thickened to a well-blended sauce.

Meanwhile, lay the fish fillets in a large skillet and add the remaining stock and wine, 1 tbsp. of the butter, and seasoning. Bring to simmering point; then poach gently until the flesh flakes when tested with the point of a knife.

Transfer the fish to a warmed serving plate and keep warm. Pour the juices from the skillet into the tomato sauce, add the remaining butter and boil to a sauce consistency. Season and pour around the fish.

Clams with Herbs and Wine
Ameîjoas à Prata

serves 4

- 4 lb. small clams
- 2 tbsp. olive oil
- 1–2 garlic cloves, crushed
- handful of mixed parsley and cilantro with a little oregano
- 1 cup well-flavored tomatoes, skinned, seeded, and chopped
- 4 tbsp. medium-bodied dry white wine
- salt and pepper

I ate this light, quick dish made with clams from the Lagoa de Obido, on the Costa de Prata. Serve with good crusty bread to mop up the delicious juices.

method

Clean, wash, and rinse the clams thoroughly.

Heat the oil in a large saucepan, add the garlic and herbs and cook, stirring frequently, for 2 minutes. Add the clams, tomatoes, and wine. Season using plenty of pepper.

Bring to a boil, then cover and cook for 3–4 minutes until the clams open.

Portuguese Fish Stew
Caldeirada de peixe

serves 4

- 6 tbsp. olive oil
- 1 fairly large onion, chopped
- 5 garlic cloves, crushed
- 3 celery stalks, chopped
- 2 leeks, chopped
- 1 small bulb Florence fennel, chopped
- 1¼ cups well-flavored tomatoes, chopped
- 2 tsp. tomato paste
- ½ red pepper, cored, seeded, and chopped
- 1 bay leaf
- 2 inch strip orange peel
- 7½ cups fish stock
- 2¼–3 lb mixed shellfish and fish (except oily varieties), filleted
- large pinch of cayenne pepper
- salt and pepper

Most coastal regions of Portugal have their own varieties of a fish stew (stew is really a misnomer as the fish only needs to be cooked gently for a short time), often containing a mixture of both white fish and shellfish. This is one that I particularly like. Use fish bones, heads, and trimmings to make the stock.

method

Heat the oil in a large saucepan. Add the onion, garlic, celery, leeks, and fennel, and cook slowly until the vegetables are very soft, about 45 minutes.

Add the tomatoes, tomato purée, red bell pepper, bay leaf, and orange peel. Cook briskly, stirring constantly, to dry out the moisture from the tomatoes.

Add the fish stock, bring to a boil and then lower the heat so the liquid simmers. Add the fish and simmer gently for 40 minutes.

Purée the mixture in batches in a blender or food processor. Pass through a sieve, if liked, pushing down well on the sieve to press through as much as possible.

Return the mixture to the pan, add the cayenne pepper and seasoning. Reheat gently.

Broiled Scabbard Fish
Espada grelhado

serves 4

- 4 scabbard or tuna fish steaks
- 1 garlic clove
- small bunch of parsley
- juice of 1 large lemon
- 3 tbsp. olive oil
- salt and pepper

Most people who have visited Madeira will have come across scabbard fish, the ugly, meter-long fish with black and white smudges on its flat body; it is the island's best-known fish. The flesh is white and moist with the texture of sole and a faint flavor of sardines. Tuna, which is also popular on Madeira, can be substituted.

method

Place the fish in a single layer in a shallow non-metallic dish.

Chop together the garlic and parsley and then mix with the lemon juice, oil, and seasoning. Pour over the fish. Leave in a cool place for about 2 hours, turning the steaks once or twice.

Preheat the broiler. Remove the fish from the marinade and grill for 3–4 minutes on each side, brushing occasionally with the marinade, until the flesh flakes easily when tested with the point of a knife.

Hake Baked in White Wine
Pescada à moda do Beira Alta

serves 4

- 1 lb potatoes, cut into chunks
- 2 cups mushrooms, quartered or sliced
- 1¼ lb well-flavored tomatoes, quartered
- 1 onion, chopped
- 1½ lb hake
- ⅔ cup medium-boiled dry white wine
- 1 tbsp. olive oil
- salt and pepper
- parsley sprigs and lemon slices, to garnish

I had this dish with some friends who make their own characterful white Dão wines.

method

Preheat the oven to 375°.

Parboil the potatoes for 5 minutes. Drain and put into an ovenproof dish with the other vegetables. Put the fish on top and pour over the wine and oil. Season and cover with foil.

Bake for 30–40 minutes until the flesh flakes easily. Serve garnished with parsley sprigs and lemon slices.

Broiled Jumbo Shrimp with Rice and Tomato Sauce
Lagosta à moda de Peniche

The fishing port of Peniche, near Cabo Carvoeiro on the coast above Lisbon, is famed for its shellfish, particularly spiny lobster, jumbo shrimp (also known as scampi) and large shrimp, which could also be used for this recipe.

method

To make the sauce, cook the onion and garlic in the oil until softened but not colored. Stir in the tomatoes and cook for a few minutes before adding the bouquet garni, wine, and olives. Simmer gently until it has thickened.

Meanwhile, cook the onion and rice in the butter, stirring, until golden. Add water to cover generously and bring to a boil. Then cover the pan and simmer for about 12 minutes until tender.

Preheat the broiler.

Thread the shrimp on skewers, brush with oil and broil for 7–8 minutes, turning occasionally.

Drain the rice, rinse quickly with boiling water and stir in the parsley and seasoning.

Season the sauce and discard the bouquet garni. Serve the shrimp on a bed of rice, accompanied by the sauce.

serves 4
- 1 onion, finely chopped
- 1⅔ cups long-grain rice
- 3 tbsp. butter
- 1½ lb. raw jumbo shrimp or large shrimp in their shells
- olive oil for brushing
- salt and pepper
- about 2–3 tbsp. chopped parsley

sauce
- 1 onion, chopped
- 1 garlic clove, chopped
- 1½ tbsp. oil
- 1¼ lb. well-flavored tomatoes, seeded, and chopped
- 1 bouquet garni
- ⅔ cup medium-bodied dry white wine
- 12 oil-cured pitted black olives

Fried Hake
Pescado frito

Being great fish eaters, the Portuguese know how to cook fish well. When frying fish they dip the pieces in beaten egg, which gives them a delicious, light, crisp coating that keeps the flesh moist.

method

Put the fish into a large, shallow, non-metallic dish. Mix together the garlic, parsley, and lemon juice and pour over the fish. Mix thoroughly and then leave in a cool place for 30–60 minutes.

Remove the fish from the dish, pat dry and toss in the flour to coat evenly and lightly.

Season the eggs and dip the fish slices in them.

Heat the oil in a wide skillet, add the fish (in batches if necessary so the pan is not crowded) and fry until golden on both sides.

Transfer the fish to paper towels to drain. If necessary, keep warm while frying the remaining slices. Serve hot with lemon wedges.

serves 4
- 1½ lb. hake, or any firm white fish, cut into 2 inch slices
- 2 garlic cloves, crushed
- 1½ tbsp. finely chopped parsley
- 2 tbsp. lemon juice
- plain flour for coating
- 2 eggs, lightly beaten
- salt and pepper
- 4 tbsp. olive oil
- lemon wedges, to serve

Broiled Jumbo Shrimp with Rice and Tomato Sauce

Squid with Bell Peppers and Tomato

Ensopada de lulas

Cook squid gently so that it is not irrevocably toughened.

serves 4

- 2¼ lb. squid, prepared
- ½ cup olive oil
- 2 onions, finely chopped
- 1 garlic clove, crushed
- 2 red bell peppers, cored, seeded, and sliced
- 1 lb. well-flavored tomatoes, chopped
- 1 cup fish stock
- 6 tbsp. dry white wine
- salt and pepper
- 2 slices Pão (see page 113) or country bread, toasted
- 1 tbsp. chopped parsley

method

Cut the squid open into two halves; then cut across into 1 inch slices.

Heat the oil in a flameproof casserole. Add the onions, garlic, and bell peppers, and cook until softened. Stir in the tomatoes and bubble until well-blended and lightly thickened. Add the stock and wine, bring to a boil and then lower the heat. Add the squid and seasoning, cover and cook gently for 1–1½ hours, or until the squid is tender and the cooking juices have reduced to a light sauce; if necessary, remove the lid towards the end of cooking to allow the sauce to evaporate slightly.

Toast the bread, cut the slices in half and put into a warmed, deep serving dish. Pour over the squid mixture and sprinkle with parsley.

CHAPTER THREE

Meat and Poultry

~

*Meat is popular in Portugal,
often considered a treat. Livestock
was not usually bred specifically
for eating; the animals were
killed when they were mature, so
the meat was tough, usually
rendered tender through
marinading or slow cooking.
Chickens are still widely kept in
the open, living off a natural diet.
They are sold by local farmers in
the open markets. Therefore, to
achieve the most authentic results
when making Portuguese chicken
recipes, free-range, corn-fed birds
should be used.
Portugal contains much country
that is ideal for game, which
includes rabbit, and the
Portuguese, particularly the
men, are keen on shooting
and hunting.*

Rice with Chicken

Arroz com frango

serves 4

- 1 large onion, chopped
- 4 tbsp. olive oil
- 2 garlic cloves, finely chopped
- 1–2 fresh red chilis, seeded, and chopped
- 1 red bell pepper, cored, seeded, and chopped
- 4 boneless half chicken breasts, skinned and cut into thin strips
- 1⅔ cups long-grain rice
- 2½ cups chicken stock
- ½ cup medium-bodied dry white wine, or additional stock
- salt and pepper
- 8 oz. chouriço, cut into thick slices
- ⅔ cup frozen peas
- 10 oil-cured black olives, pitted and sliced
- 2 tbsp. chopped parsley

The Arabs introduced rice-growing to Portugal and vibrant green paddy fields can still be seen in the lagoons along the west coast. Adding rice is a good way of making meat go further; in this recipe, the chouriço adds extra flavor.

method

Cook the onion in the oil in a large flameproof casserole until softened. Add the garlic, chilis, red bell pepper, and chicken, and cook gently for 2–3 minutes.

Add the rice, stock, wine, and seasoning. Bring to a boil, then cover and simmer for 12 minutes.

Stir in the chouriço, peas, olives, and parsley until just mixed, then cover the casserole and cook for a further 6 minutes or until the liquid has been absorbed and the rice is tender.

Fluff up with a fork and serve immediately.

Pork and Potato Hotpot

Porco à alentejana

serves 4

- 1 oz. bacon fat
- 4 pork chops
- seasoned flour
- 2½ lb. potatoes, cut into ½ inch slices
- 2 large onions, sliced
- leaves from a small handful of parsley, chopped
- salt and pepper
- 2 cups water

Pork is particularly popular in Alentejo province, probably because of its excellence. This is said to be due to the pigs' diet of chestnuts, white truffles, and acorns from the cork oaks that grow profusely there.

method

Preheat the oven to 400°.

Heat the bacon fat. Coat the chops lightly in seasoned flour, shaking off any excess, and brown quickly in the bacon fat. Remove from the pan and reserve the fat. Lay half the potato slices in a heavy-based wide casserole, followed by half the onions, sprinkling each vegetable with parsley and seasoning. Add the chops and sprinkle with parsley. Then cover with the remaining onions and more parsley and seasoning. Finish with a neat layer of the remaining potato slices. Pour over the water, followed by the reserved fat.

Cover the casserole tightly and cook in the oven for 1 hour. Remove the covering and cook for a further 15 minutes to brown the top.

Rice with Chicken

Grilled Veal Kebabs

Espetada

serves 4

- 1¼–1½ lb. veal, cut into
  1–1¼ inch cubes
- 1–2 plump garlic cloves, crushed
- 1 bay leaf, torn in half
- small handful of parsley mixed with
  a little marjoram, chopped
- 6 tbsp. medium-bodied red or
  dry white wine
- 2 tbsp. olive oil, plus extra for brushing
- salt and pepper

As elsewhere in Portugal, in Madeira often what is sold as veal (vitela), is, in fact, young beef from a weaned calf so the meat is much darker than the almost white veal we know. It is also tougher, and on the island a customary way to tenderize it is to marinade it in wine and then cook it threaded on to bay sticks. The espetada, as the kebabs are called, are traditionally accompanied with new wine.

method

Thread the veal on to four skewers and lay in a single layer in a shallow non-metallic dish.

Mix together the garlic, herbs, wine, oil, and pepper. Pour over the veal, turn the skewers and leave in a cool place for 2 hours, turning occasionally.

Preheat the broiler.

Remove the skewers from the marinade and dry on paper towels. Brush lightly with oil and broil, turning occasionally and brushing with oil, until cooked to the degree required.

Sprinkle with salt and serve.

Lentil and Pork Stew

Lentilhas com porco

serves 6

- 1 lb. green or brown lentils
- 2 onions, chopped
- 1 carrot, chopped
- 4 garlic cloves, halved lengthwise
- 1 red bell pepper, cored, seeded, and
  chopped
- 8 oz. black pudding
- 8 oz. chouriço
- 8 oz. fresh picnic shoulder, cut
  into chunks
- 1 bay leaf, torn almost in half
- several sprigs of parsley
- ½ tsp. paprika pepper
- 2 tbsp. olive oil
- salt and pepper

This is a typical, robust and filling country dish, designed for people who have toiled hard in the open.

method

Put all the ingredients into a heavy-based flameproof casserole. Add sufficient water to cover by about 1 inch, bring to a boil and then simmer gently for 30–40 minutes until the meats and lentils are tender and there is very little surplus liquid. Top up with boiling water as necessary.

Slice the black pudding and chouriço, and return to the stew. Stir together and serve.

Pork with Clams

Lombo de porco com amêijoas

Despite the unlikely sounding combination of pork and clams, this is one of the most famous and popular of Portuguese dishes, which comes from Alentejo.

serves 6

- 2¼ lb. boneless pork tenderloin, cut into 1 inch pieces
- 2 garlic cloves, finely crushed
- 2 tbsp. Red Bell Pepper Paste (see page 113)
- 1¼ cups medium-bodied dry white wine
- 1 bay leaf
- 2 cilantro sprigs
- salt and pepper
- 3 tbsp. bacon fat
- 1 large onion, finely chopped
- 2¼ lb. clams, scrubbed and well-washed

method

Put the pork into a non-metallic bowl. Mix the garlic into the Red Bell Pepper Paste and blend with the wine. Pour over the pork, add the herbs and seasoning, and stir gently together. Cover and refrigerate for 24 hours, turning the pork occasionally. Lift the pork from the marinade with a perforated spoon; reserve the marinade.

Heat the bacon fat in a large heavy-based flameproof casserole and cook the pork until evenly browned. Remove. Cook the onion in the same fat until softened but not colored.

Return the pork to the casserole, add the reserved marinade and bring to simmering point. Cover tightly and cook very gently for about 1 hour. Add the clams, cover and cook until the clams open – about 8–10 minutes; discard any that remain closed.

Pork with Clams

Chicken with Dried Mushrooms and Tomato Sauce

Frango com cogumelos e tomates

This is one of the few Portuguese recipes that call for mushrooms. The dried wild mushrooms add depth and robustness to the tomato sauce.

serves 4

- ¾ oz. dried ceps
- 1¼ cups hot chicken stock
- 3 tbsp. olive oil
- ½ large onion, finely chopped
- 3½ lb. chicken, cut into 8 portions
- 1 garlic clove, crushed
- ⅔ cup medium-bodied dry white wine
- 1 bouquet garni
- 1 cup canned chopped tomatoes
- salt and pepper
- chopped cilantro, to garnish

method

Soak the ceps in half the stock for 20 minutes. Meanwhile, heat the oil, add the onion and cook gently until beginning to soften. Add the chicken portions and cook until evenly browned, adding the garlic toward the end.

Pour in the wine and bubble for 2–3 minutes. Stir in the remaining stock, the bouquet garni, and tomatoes. Leave to simmer. Remove the ceps from the stock, chop and add to the casserole with the strained stock and seasoning. Cover and simmer gently for about 40 minutes. Transfer the chicken to a warmed serving dish. Boil the cooking liquid until reduced to a light sauce. Pour over the chicken and scatter with cilantro.

Rabbit with Onions
Coelho com ceboladas

In this recipe, large, mild but tasty and sweet Portuguese onions are slowly stewed to a golden sauce and sharpened by a touch of vinegar before the rabbit is added. The cooking time will depend on the age of the rabbit. Young, more tender, but less well-flavored farmed rabbit will be cooked within 45 minutes, while wild rabbit can take 1½–2 hours.

method

Put the onions into a heavy-based flameproof casserole with the oil, 3 tbsp. stock, and a sprinkling of salt. Cover and cook over a very low heat until the onions are well-reduced and golden. Increase the heat to moderate, stir in the sugar and cook for about 15 minutes, stirring frequently, until the onions are caramelized.

Preheat the oven to 300°.

If necessary, add a little stock to moisten the onions; then add the rabbit portions to the casserole. Turn them over a few times and then pour in the vinegar. Season generously with pepper and cook for about 5 minutes over a moderate heat.

Cover the casserole and transfer to the oven to cook until the rabbit portions are tender. Transfer the rabbit portions to a warmed serving plate. If necessary, adjust the flavor of the onions by adding more vinegar or sugar; then cook on the hob for a couple of minutes and pour over the rabbit.

serves 4–5

- 2¼ lb. Spanish onions, thinly sliced
- 2 tbsp. olive oil
- about 3–4 tbsp. meat stock
- pepper
- 2 tbsp. sugar
- 3¼ lb. rabbit portions
- about 4 tbsp. good red wine vinegar

Kid, or Lamb, Pot Roast
Cacarola de cabrito

Pot roasts are a popular main course in inland areas. This one, redolent with cilantro and red bell peppers, comes from Alentejo. A full-bodied wine, such as a mature Dão or red Barraida, makes a good companion to it.

method

Heat the oil in a roasting pan on the hob. Stir in the vegetables (except potatoes), herbs, and meat. Pour over the wine and port, if using, and season well. Cover and simmer gently for 20 minutes, stirring occasionally.

Preheat the oven to 375°F.

Put the potatoes around the meat and dot them with the bacon fat. Then, bake, uncovered, for 40–50 minutes, basting occasionally, until brown; add a little more wine, or water, if necessary. Sprinkle over the chopped parsley and cilantro before serving.

serves 6

- 6 tbsp. olive oil
- I large onion, chopped
- 3 garlic cloves, crushed
- I carrot, chopped
- 2 red bell peppers, seeded, and sliced
- several sprigs of parsley and cilantro
- 3½ lb. kid or leg of lamb, cut into chunks
- 2 cups red wine
- 2–3 tbsp. port (optional)
- salt and pepper
- 2¼ lb. waxy potatoes, parboiled and thickly sliced
- 2 tbsp. bacon fat
- chopped parsley and cilantro

Rabbit with Onions

Pork with Peas
Porco com ervilhas

serves 4–6
- 3 tbsp. olive oil
- I large onion, sliced
- 1¾ lb. boned leg of pork, cut into large chunks
- ⅔ cup medium-bodied dry white wine
- 2 cups shelled fresh (or frozen) peas
- salt and pepper
- 2 large eggs
- handful of finely chopped parsley

This dish really is best if made with fresh peas but, when they are not available, frozen ones will do.

method

Heat the oil in a heavy-based flameproof casserole, add the onion and fry until softened. Add the meat and cook until evenly browned. Stir in the wine and allow to bubble for a few minutes. Cover the casserole tightly and cook in the oven for 30 minutes. Stir in the peas and seasoning, cover again and cook for a further 20–25 minutes.

Stir the eggs and parsley together. Remove the casserole from the oven and stir in the eggs to thicken the pork mixture slightly. Serve.

Duck with Sausage and Ham-flavored Rice
Arroz de pato de Braga

serves 4
- 4½–5 lb. duck, quartered
- I small Spanish onion, thinly sliced
- 3 garlic cloves, chopped
- 8 oz. piece of bacon, cubed
- 8 oz. smoked garlic sausage, sliced
- about 4½ pt. chicken stock or water
- I lb. long-grain rice
- 3 tbsp. lemon juice
- salt and pepper

This classic Portuguese duck dish comes from the northern city of Braga, which was founded by the Romans in 279 BC.

method

Discard as much fat as possible from the duck and prick the skin in several places. Then fry in a heavy-based skillet over a fairly high heat, skin-side down, for about 4 minutes. Turn over and fry for a further 3–4 minutes. Remove to a large flameproof casserole.

Pour off most of the fat from the pan, then add the onion and cook slowly until softened and lightly colored. Stir in the garlic, bacon, and sausage, and cook over a moderate heat until the bacon is cooked. Transfer to the casserole with the duck.

Add some of the stock to the skillet, bring to a boil, stirring and pour over the duck. Add just enough extra stock to cover the duck. Bring to a boil, cover and cook gently for about 1½ hours.

Remove the duck, discard the skin, cover and keep warm. Strain the stock through a sieve. Reserve the contents of the sieve. Remove as much fat as possible from the stock. Measure 4¼ cups stock; make up with water if necessary.

Put the rice into the casserole, put the duck and contents of the sieve on top and pour over the stock. Add the lemon juice and seasoning. Bring to a boil, then cover and simmer gently for about 20 minutes or until the rice is tender.

Chicken Piri-piri
Frango Piri-piri

serves 6
- oil for frying
- 6 chicken portions
- 2 onions, sliced into rings
- 6 tomatoes, chopped
- 2 carrots, cut into sticks
- 1 large parsnip, cut into sticks
- 1 cinnamon stick
- salt and pepper
- Piri-piri (see page 110)
- 1 large red bell pepper, cored, seeded, and thinly sliced
- 1 large yellow bell pepper, cored, seeded, and thinly sliced

Take care when adding Piri-piri as it can be very hot; the strength of the homemade sauce will depend on the fieriness of the chilis you have used. If you do not have any homemade Piri-piri it is possible to buy it from specialist Portuguese food stores, or hot pepper sauce can be substituted.

method

Heat the oil in a large flameproof casserole. Add the chicken portions, in batches if necessary, and brown evenly. Add the onions, tomatoes, carrots, parsnip, cinnamon, seasoning, and 3 cups water.

Bring the contents of the casserole to a boil, stir in a little Piri-piri, cover and simmer gently for 30 minutes.

Add the bell peppers to the casserole, cover again and continue to simmer gently for 30 minutes, or until the chicken and vegetables are tender.

Using a perforated spoon, transfer the chicken and vegetables to a warmed serving dish. Keep warm.

Boil the cooking liquid rapidly until reduced by about a third. Taste and add more Piri-piri if necessary. Pour the sauce over the chicken and vegetables and serve.

Jugged Chicken
Frango na pucara

serves 4
- 4½ oz. smoked ham, cut into 4 slices
- 4 chicken portions
- 12 small onions, peeled
- 4 tomatoes, seeded and quartered
- 1 red bell pepper, cored, seeded, and sliced
- 3 garlic cloves, crushed
- 1¼ cups medium-bodied dry white wine
- 2 tbsp. Dijon-style mustard
- 4 tbsp. brandy
- 4 tbsp. tawny or white port
- salt and pepper
- small handful of chopped parsley, to serve

A pucara is an earthenware cooking pot or jug used for cooking chicken and mature game. The pucara is covered and left to cook very gently and slowly (mature game and traditional Portuguese chickens need such cooking to tenderize them) so the meat and flavorings steam and stew together; the cooking time below has been adjusted to suit regular chickens. The flavor of Jugged Chicken is pronounced.

method

Preheat the oven to 325°.

Lay the ham slices in a heavy-based deep casserole. Put the chicken portions on top and tuck the vegetables around.

Blend the wine into the mustard and pour over the chicken. Add the brandy and port. Season, cover very tightly and cook in the oven for 1½–2 hours. Scatter the parsley over the chicken and serve.

Pork Steaks Marinated in Olive Oil with Mint, and Broiled

Bifes de porco grelhado

The meat can also be cubed and threaded on skewers with cubes of red pepper as illustrated.

serves 4

- 4 pork steaks
- salt and pepper

Marinade

- 1 onion, chopped
- 1 garlic clove, chopped
- leaves from a bunch of mint (about 1½–2 oz.)
- 2 tbsp. lemon juice
- ⅔ cup extra virgin olive oil

method

Season the pork with pepper and lay in a shallow non-metallic dish.

To make the marinade, blend the onion, garlic, mint, lemon juice, and oil to a paste and spread over the meat. Cover and leave in a cool place or the refrigerator for 6–8 hours, turning the meat a few times.

Preheat the broiler.

Broil the pork for 5–6 minutes on each side, sprinkle with salt and serve with crusty bread and a green salad.

Pork Steaks Marinated in Olive Oil, with Mint, and Broiled

Rabbit in Red Wine
Coelho à Beira

The authentic wine to use is a red Dão, the best-known Portuguese red table wine. It is smooth, fruity, and full-bodied, so makes this a robust rabbit dish. There is no problem about the choice of wine to serve with the dish – the same that has been used in the cooking.

serves 4

- 1 rabbit, jointed
- 2 onions, chopped
- 3 garlic cloves, crushed
- 5 oz. presunto or bacon, chopped
- 2 tbsp. olive oil
- 1 tsp. all-purpose flour
- 1 cup light game, chicken, or veal stock
- 1 cup red wine
- bouquet garni
- salt and pepper
- chopped parsley, to garnish

method

Cook the rabbit portions, onions, garlic, and presunto or bacon in the olive oil in a heavy flameproof casserole, until the rabbit portions are brown and the onions softened. Remove the rabbit portions.

Sprinkle the flour over the onion mixture and stir it in for 1–2 minutes. Pour in the stock slowly, stirring constantly, then add the wine and bring to a boil. Simmer for 2–3 minutes before returning the rabbit portions to the casserole with the bouquet garni and seasoning. Cover tightly and cook gently until the rabbit is tender.

Discard the bouquet garni, sprinkle with chopped parsley and serve.

Lisbon Liver

Iscas

serves 4

- 1 lb. lamb liver, thinly sliced
- 4 garlic cloves, crushed
- 1 bay leaf
- salt and pepper
- ¾ cup dry white wine
- 1 tbsp. white wine vinegar
- 3 tbsp. shortening or olive oil
- 2 oz. presunto, prosciutto, or bacon, chopped

Thinly sliced liver which is marinated, then cooked with presunto, is traditionally associated with Lisbon, but is popular throughout Portugal.

method

Put the liver into a dish, add the garlic, bay leaf, and seasoning, and pour over the wine and vinegar. Cover and leave in a cool place for at least 4 hours, preferably overnight.

Remove the liver from the wine and pat dry with paper towels. Reserve the wine, discarding the bay leaf.

Heat the shortening or oil, add the ham or bacon and cook until crisp. Add the liver and cook for about 3 minutes on each side. Transfer the liver and ham or bacon to a warmed plate, cover and keep warm.

Stir the wine into the pan and boil rapidly until reduced by about half. Pour over the liver.

Marinated Roast Veal

Trouxa de vitela

serves 6–8

- about 3½ lb. joint of lean, boneless veal, such as top of leg or rump
- ⅞ cup olive oil
- 4 tbsp. white wine vinegar
- 1 large red onion, finely chopped
- 1 garlic clove, crushed
- 1 red chili, seeded and chopped
- 2½ tbsp. chopped parsley
- salt and pepper

Portuguese veal is redder and more full-flavored than we are accustomed to, but this recipe works very well with the veal available to us as the marinade moistens the lean flesh and adds flavor to it.

method

Put the veal in a non-metallic deep dish that it just fits comfortably. Mix together ⅔ cup of the oil and the remaining ingredients. Pour over the veal, turn the meat, then cover and leave in a cool place for 4 hours, or in the refrigerator for 8, turning occasionally.

Preheat the oven to 450°.

Put the veal on a rack in a roasting pan and brush off any piece of herb, garlic or chili. Reserve the marinade.

Roast the meat for 20 minutes. Pour over 1 tbsp. or so of the remaining oil, lower the oven temperature to 350° and roast for about 1½ hours, basting a few more times with the cooking juices and remaining oil. Leave to rest for 15 minutes in the oven with the heat turned off and the door propped open.

Bring the remaining marinade to a boil in a small saucepan and simmer for 5 minutes.

Slice the veal and pour the marinade over the slices.

Braised Shoulder of Lamb

Borrego estufado

serves 4–6

- 3½ lb. lamb shoulder, boned
- 1 garlic head, peeled
- salt and pepper
- ½ tsp. ground dried thyme
- 4 carrots, chopped
- 2 celery stalks, chopped
- 4 onions, chopped
- 2 leeks, chopped
- 5 cups lamb stock
- 1 cup well-flavored tomatoes, skinned, seeded, and chopped
- 1 tbsp. chopped mixed herbs, such as parsley, cilantro, and mint

The lamb that is cooked in Portugal tends to come from older animals than we are used to. Consequently it is tougher and benefits from long, slow cooking. The vegetables will be very soft by the end of cooking, but can be served with the meat if liked. Use the bones to make the stock.

method

Preheat the oven to 300°.

Open out the lamb and trim it. Crush 2–3 of the garlic cloves with a pinch of salt and mix with the thyme and pepper. Rub well into the cut surface of the meat. Tie the meat back into shape and season.

Put the lamb into a deep, heavy-based casserole with the remaining garlic and the vegetables, except the tomatoes. Pour over the stock and bring to a boil. Cover the casserole tightly and cook in the oven for about 3½ hours until very tender.

Transfer the meat to a warmed serving plate and leave to rest in the oven with the heat turned off and the door propped open slightly.

Meanwhile, strain the stock from the casserole, measure off 1¼ cups and skim the fat from the surface. Keep the vegetables warm with the meat, if liked.

Simmer the tomatoes in the 1¼ cups stock until softened. Stir in the herbs, and seasoning if necessary.

Cut the lamb into thick slices and serve with the sauce.

Pork Casserole with Cumin

Rojões do Minho

serves 4

- 1½ lb. boneless lean pork, cut into 1½ inch pieces
- 1½ tsp. ground cumin
- 3 garlic cloves, crushed
- 1 bay leaf
- salt and pepper
- ⅓ cup dry white wine
- 2 tsp. lemon juice
- 2 tbsp. olive oil
- 1 onion, finely chopped
- 10–12 pitted black olives
- lemon wedges, to serve

Rojões is the local Minho name for pork stew, or casserole. The cumin, underlaid with lemon, gives a subtle exotic flavor to the dish.

method

Put the pork into a mixing bowl and add the cumin, garlic, bay leaf, and seasoning. Pour over the wine and lemon juice. Stir to mix, then cover and leave in the refrigerator for 6–8 hours, stirring a few times.

Preheat oven to 325°.

Drain the pork from the marinade, reserving the marinade.

Heat the oil in a heavy-based flameproof casserole, add the onion and cook until softened. Add the pork and fry until browned, stirring occasionally. Stir in the reserved marinade, cover and cook in the oven for 1–1½ hours until the pork is tender. Scatter over the olives and serve with lemon wedges.

Marinated Pork with Fried Cornbread

Carne de vinho e alhos, e milho frito

This recipe comes from Madeira, where fried cornbread is a specialty.

method

Put the pork into a non-metallic dish and add the garlic, coriander, and seasoning. Pour over the wine, stir, cover and leave in a cool place, or the refrigerator, for several hours or overnight.

Drain the pork from the marinade, reserving the marinade. Pat the pork dry with paper towels. Heat 2 tbsp. of the oil in a heavy-based pan, and fry the pork until evenly sealed. Using a perforated spoon, transfer to a bowl.

Lower the heat, add another 2 tbsp. of the oil and the onion, and cook until they have softened and are beginning to brown. Stir in the paprika for 30–60 seconds, then stir in the pork to coat thoroughly with the onion mixture.

Pour in the marinade, bring to a boil, then cover and simmer gently for 20–25 minutes until the pork is almost tender. Uncover and continue cooking until the pork is tender and the liquid reduced.

Meanwhile, heat the remaining oil in a large skillet, add the bread and fry until golden on both sides.

Serve the pork with, or on top of, the fried bread.

serves 4–6

- 2¼ lb. boneless shoulder of pork, cut into 1 inch cubes
- 2 garlic cloves, chopped
- 2 tsp. coriander seeds, crushed
- salt and pepper
- ½ bottle medium-bodied dry white wine
- about 6 tbsp. olive oil
- 1 large onion, sliced
- 1 tsp. paprika
- 4–6 slices Cornbread (see page 114)

VINDIMANDO

Painted tile scene showing vine cultivation on the steep slopes of the Douro.

Chicken Baked with Potatoes and Garlic

Frango à moda do alentejana

An extremely easy dish to make and cook, and based on simple ingredients. It is also delicious to eat, provided that good potatoes and a fresh free-range chicken are used, as they would be in Portugal. Don't be put off by the amount of garlic – the flavor mellows to a mild creaminess during the cooking.

serves 6

- 3½ lb. chicken, cut into 12–16 pieces
- 2¼ lb. yellow waxy potatoes, quartered
- 1 onion, sliced
- 20 small–medium sprigs of rosemary
- salt and pepper
- 8 tbsp. olive oil
- 20 unpeeled garlic cloves

method

Preheat the oven to 425°.

Put the chicken, potatoes, onion, rosemary, and seasoning into a large, shallow baking dish. Mix together and then pour over the oil. Scatter the garlic cloves over the top and bake for 20 minutes.

Lower the oven temperature to 375° and bake for about 45 minutes, turning the chicken and potatoes occasionally, until the chicken is cooked, the potatoes golden and the garlic crisp.

Chicken Baked with Potatoes and Garlic

Braised Rabbit with Potatoes and Artichokes
Coelho Madeira

If using wild rabbit, which has more flavor than farmed rabbit, use a young animal as an older one may dominate the taste of new potatoes and artichokes.

serves 4-6

- 1 6 medium large globe artichokes
- ½ lemon
- 2 tbsp. olive oil
- 1 young rabbit, jointed
- 1 small onion, finely chopped
- ⅔ cup dry white wine
- 1 lb. new potatoes
- 1 tbsp. finely chopped parsley
- salt and pepper
- chopped parsley to garnish

Snap off the artichoke stems. Using a small sharp knife, pare off the top part of the leaves to leave the tender inner cone. Pull away the cone and cut off the hairy "choke". Cut the bases into halves or quarters. Squeeze the lemon into a bowl of water and add the artichokes.

Heat the oil in a wide heavy-based flameproof casserole. Add the rabbit portions and fry until an even light golden brown. Transfer to a plate. Add the onion to the casserole and cook gently until soft but not brown. Stir in the wine, and bring to a boil. Return the rabbit portions to the casserole. Add the parsley and seasoning, cover and cook gently for about 15 minutes. Add the potatoes, cover again and cook for 15 minutes.

Add the artichokes to the casserole. Cover and cook for a further 25 minutes, shaking the casserole occasionally. Make sure the casserole does not dry out. Sprinkle with parsley.

Portuguese Steak with Onions
Bife de cebolada

This recipe for fried steak was an old favorite on restaurant menus because the beef that most people bought for cooking at home was so tough it had to be stewed. The dish is traditionally served with Portuguese Fried Potatoes (page 93).

method

Using a mortar and pestle or the end of a rolling pin in a small bowl, mash 2 of the garlic cloves with a pinch of salt; then mix in the vinegar and black pepper. Rub into both sides of each steak. Leave in a cool place for 30 minutes.

Halve the remaining garlic. Heat the oil in a large heavy-based skillet, add the garlic halves and the bay leaf, and cook for 1–1½ minutes, stirring. Using a perforated spoon, discard the garlic and bay leaf. Add the steaks and brown quickly and evenly on both sides – 2–3 minutes a side. Transfer to warmed plates and keep warm.

Pour off most of the fat from the pan, then add the ham and cook, stirring, for 2 minutes. Stir in the wine, dislodging the sediment, and boil until lightly thickened. Season and pour over the steaks. Serve sprinkled with the parsley.

serves 4
- 4 plump garlic cloves
- salt and pepper
- 2½ tsp. red wine vinegar
- 4 steaks, about ¾ inch thick
- 3 tbsp. olive oil
- I large bay leaf, torn in half
- 4 oz. presunto ham, chopped
- 6 tbsp. full-bodied red wine
- I tbsp. chopped parsley

Braised Partridge
Perdiz à Guincho

The beach at Guincho, northwest of Lisbon, is a weekend playground for Lisboans in summer, but in the autumn men in particular turn their attention to the heath behind the beach to indulge their love of shooting.

method

Preheat the oven to 400°.

Season the partridge inside and out and brush liberally with oil. Roast the birds for 14–16 minutes, first on one side, then on the other, turning halfway through. Meanwhile, cut the core from the cabbages and coarsely shred the leaves.

Heat a little oil in a deep, heavy-based flameproof casserole. Add the presunto or bacon and cook over a medium heat, stirring, for 3 minutes. Stir in the onion, carrots, and celery, and cook for a further 3 minutes until they begin to color. Then add the cabbage. Lower the heat, cover the casserole and cook for 5 minutes. Stir in the juniper berries and pepper, cover again and cook for a further 5 minutes. Push the partridge, breast-sides up, down into the cabbage so they are half-buried. Pour over the stock, cover the birds with oiled foil and return to the oven for about 25 minutes.

serves 4
- 4 dressed partridge
- salt and pepper
- olive oil
- 2 Savoy cabbages, halved
- 8 oz. piece presunto or lightly smoked bacon, cut into strips
- I large onion, chopped
- ¾ cup diced carrots
- 2 celery stalks, diced
- 6 juniper berries
- I¼ cups game or chicken stock

Portuguese Steak with Onions

Charcoal-grilled Chicken

Frango no churrasco

serves 4

- 1 garlic clove, crushed
- 5 tbsp. dry white wine
- about ½ tsp. paprika
- Piri-piri (see page 110) or hot pepper sauce
- salt and pepper
- 4 chicken portions

Food cooked over charcoal is always in demand, especially in the open air and in the south of Portugal, not only for the delicious flavor it acquires during cooking, but also because of the informal, convivial atmosphere associated with it.

method

Mix the garlic and wine with paprika, Piri-piri or hot pepper sauce, and seasoning to taste.

Slash each chicken portion three times and arrange in a single layer in a shallow dish. Spoon over the wine mixture, rubbing it in well. Cover and leave in a cool place for 2 hours, turning occasionally.

Preheat a barbecue or broiler.

Remove the chicken from the dish and cook on the barbecue or broiler for about 25 minutes until the juices run clear, turning twice and basting with any remaining wine mixture.

The Basilica of St. Lucia in Viana do Castelo – the capital of Portuguese folklore, famous for its colorful costumes, embroidery, filigree jewellery, and ceramics.

CHAPTER FOUR

Vegetables and Salads

~

The vegetables grown in
Portugal are a mixture of those
that are indigenous, such as peas
and fava beans, and those that
were brought back from the
Americas by the explorers, such
as bell peppers, chilis, tomatoes,
and potatoes, a great Portuguese
favorite. Vegetables are often
combined to make quite
substantial dishes and can
therefore either form filling
accompaniments to meat,
poultry, or fish dishes, so
reducing the amount of the main
course, or they can be served as a
main course in themselves.
Salads are particularly good in
the south, where such excellent
ingredients for them flourish.

Tomato and Cheese Salad

Salada de tomate com queijos

serves 4
- 1¼ lb. well-flavored tomatoes, sliced
- 4 oz. sheep's cheese, coarsely chopped or sliced
- chopped cilantro

to serve
- olive oil
- 2 lemons, halved
- salt and pepper

The slight tang of a semi-hard sheep's cheese makes a good contrast to cool, sweet and juicy tomatoes, and chopped cilantro complements them both to make one of the best tomato salads I know.

method

Arrange the tomato slices in a shallow bowl and scatter the cheese on top. Sprinkle with chopped cilantro and serve with the oil, lemon halves, and seasoning for each person to add their own, in that order.

Braised Lentils

Le estufado

serves 4
- 2 tbsp. olive oil
- 1 onion, finely chopped
- 1 plump garlic clove, crushed
- 1 leek, chopped
- 1 carrot, chopped
- 1 potato, chopped
- 1 large tomato, peeled and chopped
- generous 1 cup brown lentils
- 2½ cups veal, chicken, or vegetable stock
- 1 bouquet garni
- 2 anchovy fillets, chopped
- 2 tsp. wine vinegar
- salt and pepper

The theory is that if a large, steaming bowl of these well-flavored lentils accompanies a meat dish, the amount of meat eaten will be reduced. The lentils are so good that the theory is always accurate.

method

Heat the oil in a saucepan, add the onion and cook until softened and lightly colored. Stir in the garlic, leek, carrot, and potato, and cook for 4–5 minutes. Stir in the tomato, followed by the lentils a minute or so later.

When everything is mixed together, add the stock and bouquet garni, bring to a boil and simmer for 30–40 minutes until the lentils and vegetables are tender.

Discard the bouquet garni. Purée about one-third of the lentil mixture with the anchovy fillets and vinegar in a blender. Return to the pan, reheat and season.

Tomato and Cheese Salad

Fava Beans with Cilantro

Favas com coentro

serves 4

- 2 oz. piece of bacon, cut into strips
- 1 onion, finely chopped
- 1 lb. shelled fresh or thawed frozen fava beans
- salt and pepper
- 2 tomatoes, peeled, seeded, and chopped
- ¾ cup chopped cilantro

A liberal amount of chopped cilantro, and some chopped tomato stirred into the beans just before serving, makes this a particularly interesting and memorable way of serving fava beans.

method

Cook the bacon in a heavy saucepan until the fat runs. Stir in the onion and cook until softened. Add the beans, barely cover with water and simmer until they are tender, 6–15 minutes depending on the age of the beans; or cook according to the directions on the package if using frozen beans.

Strain the beans and return to the pan. Stir in the seasoning and tomatoes, cover and heat gently, shaking the pan occasionally, for a few minutes to warm the tomatoes. Stir in the cilantro and serve.

Grilled Tomato Salad with Red Bell Peppers

Salada de tomate assado

The tomatoes and peppers can be charred over a barbecue, as is often done in the Algarve, from where this salad comes. Two or three unpeeled garlic cloves can also be grilled, then either crushed and used in the dressing, or sliced and mixed with the tomatoes and peppers.

method

Preheat the barbecue or broiler.

Grill the tomatoes and bell peppers, turning frequently, until evenly charred and blistered. Leave until cool enough to handle and then peel them.

Slice the tomatoes. Cut the bell peppers in half and discard the cores and seeds; then slice the flesh.

Mix together the tomatoes and bell peppers. Whisk together the oil, vinegar, garlic, and seasoning, pour over the vegetables and leave for about 1 hour.

Serve sprinkled with cilantro or parsley.

serves 4

- 1¼ lb. firm, but ripe, well-flavored tomatoes
- 2 red bell peppers
- 6 tbsp. olive oil
- 1½ tbsp. mild red wine vinegar
- 1 garlic clove, crushed
- salt and pepper
- chopped cilantro or parsley, to serve

Potato and Tomato Pie
Bola de batata e tomate

Two of Portugal's favorite vegetables are brought together in this simple yet tasty recipe from the Douro. It makes a good supper or lunch dish, or a vegetarian main course, and is a useful way of using leftover cooked potatoes.

serves 4

- about 6 boiled or steamed medium-sized potatoes, thinly sliced
- Red Bell Pepper Paste (see page 113), for spreading
- 1 bunch of parsley
- 1 garlic clove
- 1 fresh red chili, seeded
- 3 tbsp. virgin olive oil, plus extra for trickling
- squeeze of lemon juice
- salt and pepper
- 1¼ lb. well-flavored tomatoes, skinned, seeded, and sliced

method

Preheat the oven to 400°.

Lay the potato slices in a well-oiled, shallow baking dish. Spread thinly with Red Bell Pepper Paste.

Chop the parsley, garlic, and chili together and mix with the oil. Add lemon juice and seasoning to taste and spread half over the potatoes. Cover with the tomatoes and spoon over the remaining parsley mixture. Trickle over a little oil and bake for 30–40 minutes. Serve warm, not straight from the oven.

Portuguese Fried Potatoes
Batatas à Portuguesa

*Fried potatoes accompany many Portuguese main courses; when they are served
with Lisbon Liver (see page 74) or Portuguese Steak with Onions (see page 81)
they are traditionally arranged in a ring around the meat.*

method

Heat the oil over a moderate heat in a large, heavy-based skillet. Add
the potatoes and cook for about 15 minutes until tender and golden,
turning the slices frequently so they cook evenly.

Season the potatoes, drain on paper towels and transfer to a warm
serving dish. Sprinkle with parsley and serve immediately.

serves 4
- 4 tbsp. olive oil
- 1½ lb. small potatoes, sliced into
  ¼ inch thick rings
- salt and pepper
- finely chopped parsley

Peas with Chouriço and Eggs
Ervilhas à Algarvia

*Topped with a poached, or sometimes fried, egg, this southern Portuguese dish
of peas spiced with chouriço and red pepper can be served for lunch or supper.
If the eggs are omitted, the flavored peas make an accompaniment to roast
or broiled chicken.*

method

Heat the oil and chouriço in a saucepan for 2–3 minutes; then add
the onion, garlic, and red bell pepper. Cook gently until the vegetables
are tender.

Stir in the peas and seasoning for 1 minute then barely cover with
water. Simmer gently until tender, 10–20 minutes depending on the age
of the peas; or cook according to the directions on the package if using
frozen peas.

Meanwhile, heat water in a wide skillet to just on simmering point.
Crack in the eggs gently, baste the yolks with water and poach until
cooked to your liking.

Drain the peas, mix in the cilantro and tip into a warm serving dish.
Using a perforated spoon, remove the eggs from the water and place on
top of the peas. Season the eggs and serve.

serves 4
- 2 tbsp. olive oil
- 4 oz. chouriço, chopped
- 1 onion, finely chopped
- 1–2 plump garlic cloves, finely chopped
- 1 red bell pepper, seeded and chopped
- 1½ lb. shelled fresh or thawed frozen
  peas
- salt and pepper
- 4 eggs
- ¾ cup chopped cilantro

Peas with Chouriço and Eggs

Mixed Salad
Uma salada à Portuguesa

serves 2

- 3 tbsp. olive oil
- 1 tbsp. lemon juice
- salt and pepper
- 1 head round lettuce
- several leaves of chicory
- 1 bunch of watercress
- 1 large well-flavored tomato, thinly sliced
- 1 red onion, thinly sliced and separated into rings
- 8 oil-cured black olives (optional)

A simple lettuce, tomato, and onion salad is a frequent sight on dining tables, either as a light appetizer or an accompaniment to the main course.

method

Whisk together the oil, lemon juice, and seasoning.

Tear the lettuce and chicory leaves into small pieces and toss with the watercress; then toss lightly with the dressing.

Put the salad leaves into a bowl. Arrange the tomato slices overlapping on top, scatter over the onion rings and olives, if using, and serve.

Potatoes with Tomato Sauce
Batatas com tomatada

serves 4

- 1½ lb. potatoes, boiled and sliced
- ½ quantity tomato sauce (see page 112)
- 4 tbsp. mixed bread crumbs and finely grated Cheddar cheese
- black pepper
- chopped cilantro or parsley to serve

Serve with roast or broiled meat or poultry.

method

Preheat the oven to 350°.

Arrange the potato slices in a shallow baking dish and pour over the sauce.

Season the bread crumbs mixture with black pepper and sprinkle evenly over the sauce. Bake for about 15-20 minutes until the top is brown, Sprinkle with chopped cilantro or parsley to serve.

Cobbler in Lisbon. Several trades in Portugal remain largely unmodernized and still rely on traditional tools and methods.

Mixed Salad

Garbanzo Bean Stew
Cozido de grão à Barcelos

Garbanzo beans are eaten so frequently they are sold from, and indeed by, the sackful in open markets. Being cheap, nutritious and filling, they are often added to casseroles and stews to "stretch" the meat content.

Barcelos is an historic town in the Minho, famous for its pottery cocks. According to the legend of their origin, a pilgrim on his way to the holy shrine of St James at Santiago de Compostella in Spain was falsely accused and convicted of theft. Condemned to be hanged, he invoked St James and, noticing that his judge was dining off roast cockerel, declared that the bird should stand up and crow as proof of his innocence. It did, and he was duly released.

method

Put the garbanzo beans into a saucepan and just cover with water. Bring to a boil, then cover and simmer while preparing the remaining ingredients.

Heat the oil in another saucepan, add the presunto or bacon, and pork and chouriço, and brown evenly. Remove using a perforated spoon. Stir the onion, garlic, carrot, celery, and leek into the pan and fry until softened and lightly browned.

Stir some of the water from the garbanzo beans into the onion mixture to dislodge the sediment on the bottom of the pan. Then add the remaining water and the beans. Return the meats to the pan and add the bouquet garni and stock. Simmer gently, partly covered, for about 1¼ hours until the garbanzo beans and pork are tender. There should only be a little water left in the pan at the end of cooking; if necessary, leave the pan uncovered so that the excess water will evaporate, or add more water if the pan becomes dry.

Discard the bouquet garni, season and stir in the parsley before serving.

serves 4–6

- 1 cup garbanzo beans, soaked overnight and drained
- 2 tbsp. olive oil
- 4 oz. piece of presunto or smoked bacon, cut into strips
- 1 lb. pork shoulder, cubed
- 5 oz. chouriço, thickly sliced
- 1 large onion, chopped
- 2 plump garlic cloves, chopped
- 1 carrot, chopped
- 1 celery stalk, chopped
- 1 leek, chopped
- 1 bouquet garni
- 1 cup vegetable, veal, or brown veal stock
- salt and pepper
- handful of chopped parsley

Navy Beans with Tomato Sauce and Onion
Feijão com tomatada e cebola

serves 4

- 8 oz. navy beans, soaked overnight and drained
- 3 tbsp. virgin olive oil
- 3 garlic cloves, finely chopped
- 3 tbsp. chopped parsley
- 1 tbsp. chopped mixed thyme and rosemary
- 1 bay leaf
- pinch of dried oregano
- ¼–½ tsp. crushed red pepper flakes
- 1 cup water
- 2 large tomatoes, peeled, seeded, and diced
- salt and pepper
- ¼ Spanish onion, very finely chopped
- finely chopped cilantro or parsley, to serve

This recipe is distinguished from other beans in tomato sauce recipes by the addition of a mound of finely chopped raw onion and some chopped cilantro or parsley to each portion as it is served. This really livens up the dish, but it is important to use a mild onion.

method

Put the beans into a saucepan and just cover with water. Boil for 10 minutes and then simmer for about 50 minutes or until the beans are tender.

Heat the oil, garlic, herbs, and crushed red pepper gently for 4 minutes. Add the water, bring to a boil, then cover and simmer for 5 minutes. Stir in the tomatoes, cover again and simmer for 4 minutes.

Drain the beans and stir into the tomato mixture gently. Season and simmer for 4–5 minutes.

Ladle the beans and sauce into four warmed soup plates and put a small mound of onion and some cilantro or parsley in the center of each.

Potatoes with Bacon and Onion
Batatas à moda do alentejana

This interesting potato dish can be served with simply cooked chicken, with regular omelets or scrambled eggs, or can be topped with poached eggs.

method
Boil the potatoes until tender. Drain thoroughly and slice.

Meanwhile, fry the onion in the oil until softened but not colored. Remove and keep warm.

Add the bacon to the pan and cook until brown and crisp. Add the potatoes and cook until browned on both sides.

Stir the onion, cilantro or parsley, and seasoning into the potatoes gently. Warm through and serve.

serves 4–6
- 2¼ lb. potatoes
- 1 onion, chopped
- 3 tbsp. olive oil
- 4–6 oz. piece smoked bacon, chopped
- ¾ cup chopped cilantro or parsley
- salt and pepper

Tomato Rice

Arroz de tomate

serves 4

- 2 tbsp. olive oil
- 1 large onion, finely chopped
- 1 garlic clove, finely chopped
- 2 ripe, well-flavored tomatoes, skinned, seeded and finely chopped
- generous 1 cup long-grain rice
- boiling water
- 2 tbsp. chopped parsley
- salt and pepper

This is one of the most popular of the many Portuguese rice dishes. Much of its character come from the well-flavored, locally grown tomatoes, so choose them carefully; many stores are now selling varieties that have been grown specifically for their flavor. If the rice is still soggy at the end of cooking, it is described as malandrinho *(naughty). Serve the rice with roast, broiled or fried meat, poultry and fish, fish cakes, and omelets.*

method

Heat the oil in a saucepan, add the onion and garlic, and fry until softened but not brown.

Stir in the tomatoes, cook for a further 5 minutes or so before adding the rice. Stir to coat with the vegetables; then add boiling water to 2½ times the volume of the rice. Bring to a boil, cover and cook over a low heat until the rice is tender and all the liquid has been absorbed. Stir in the parsley and seasoning to taste.

Garbanzo Beans with Spinach

Grão com espinafres

serves 4

- 8 oz. garbanzo beans soaked overnight and drained
- 2¼ lb. spinach
- 1 large onion, thinly sliced
- 4 garlic cloves, chopped
- salt, pepper and paprika pepper
- ½ cup beef stock
- 4 tbsp. olive oil

To maintain the low heat that is necessary for this dish, I use a heat diffusing mat.

method

Cook the garbanzo beans in simmering water for about 1 hour. Drain thoroughly.

Put one-third of the spinach in a heavy flameproof casserole; cover with half the onion and garlic, then half the garbanzo beans, seasoning each layer with salt, pepper, and paprika.

Repeat the layers, ending with the remaining spinach. Pour over the stock and then pour the oil evenly over the top. Cover tightly and cook gently until the garbanzo beans are tender and there is no surplus liquid; if necessary, add more stock, or water, to prevent the mixture drying out.

Stuffed Tomatoes
Tomates recheados

These tomatoes are very versatile – they go well with roast or broiled meat or poultry, or fish; they can also be served as part of an all-vegetable meal, or as an appetizer.

serves 4

- 4 very large, ripe, well-flavored tomatoes, or 8 smaller ones, halved horizontally
- 2 handfuls fresh bread crumbs
- 2 garlic cloves, finely chopped
- handful of chopped parsley
- 3 tbsp. olive oil
- 2 eggs, beaten
- salt and pepper

method

Scoop out the insides of the tomatoes carefully. Season the inside of the tomatoes, turn them upside down and leave to drain.

Mix together the remaining ingredients. Place the tomatoes the right way up in a greased baking dish and fill with the bread crumb mixture.

Bake at 400° for about 15 minutes. Serve hot.

Overlooking the beautiful rolling countryside from the Capela Sao Gens Serra.

The beautiful botanical gardens, Lisbon, renowned for their imaginative landscaping.

Fava Bean Salad
Favas frescas em salada

serves 4
- 1 lb. shelled fresh or frozen fava beans
- 1 garlic clove, unpeeled
- 3 tbsp. olive oil
- 1 tbsp. white wine vinegar
- salt and pepper

to garnish
- 1 hard-cooked egg, cut into wedges
- chopped cilantro

Boiling the garlic for a short time gives it a more mellow flavor so there is only a subtle garlic taste to the dish.

method

Cook the fava beans in boiling water until tender, adding the garlic 3 minutes before the beans are ready.

Meanwhile, whisk the oil, vinegar, and seasoning together. Drain the beans and garlic. Peel the garlic; crush and whisk with the dressing.

While the beans are still warm, toss with the dressing and then leave to cool completely.

Serve garnished with hard-cooked egg and sprinkled with cilantro.

Tomato Salad
Salada de tomate

serves 4
- 1¼ lb. well-flavored tomatoes, skinned, seeded, and chopped
- 1 red onion, finely chopped
- 3 tbsp. olive oil
- 1 tbsp. white wine vinegar
- 2 tsp. chopped oregano
- salt and pepper

As the white onions most usually on sale rarely have the mild sweetness of Portuguese ones, I often use red onions for salads.

method

Toss together the tomatoes and onion.

Whisk together the oil, white wine vinegar, oregano, and seasoning. Pour over the vegetables and toss lightly. Cover and chill well.

Sautéed Greens
Grelos

Grelos *is derived from the Portuguese verb* greler, *meaning "to sprout", indicating that the green part of any sprouting vegetable could be used – for example, kale, Swiss chard, spinach, spring greens, beet, or turnip leaves.*

serves 4
- 4 tbsp. olive oil
- 3–4 plump garlic cloves, crushed
- 2¼ lb. young greens
- salt and pepper

method
Heat the oil in a large saucepan, add the garlic and cook until softened but do not allow to brown.

Stir in the greens and cook over a moderately high heat for about 4 minutes – the volume will decrease as they cook. Stir in seasoning and serve immediately.

Navy Beans with Tomatoes
Feijão branco à moda de Beira

Sliced chouriço, salt pork or bacon can be added to make a more substantial dish.

serves 4–6
- 1 lb. navy beans, soaked overnight and drained
- 1 lb. well-flavored tomatoes, chopped
- ¼–½ cup olive oil
- 3 garlic cloves, halved lengthwise
- 3 bay leaves
- small handful of parsley
- salt and pepper

method
Put the beans into a saucepan and just cover with water. Boil for 10 minutes, then cover and cook very gently until the beans are just tender – the time will depend on how fresh they are.

Drain the beans and mix the remaining ingredients. Continue to cook very gently for about 1 hour until the sauce is very thick and the beans on the point of disintegration. Discard the herbs and serve.

The infamous Discoverers' Monument, Lisbon, celebrating the discovery of The New World.

Fava Beans with Bacon and Herbs
Favas à Portuguesa

Fava beans are popular fresh vegetables in summer. More than enough for immediate consumption are grown so the surplus can be dried to provide a staple winter food for country dwellers.

serves 4

- 4 oz. piece of bacon, cut into strips
- 1 onion, chopped
- 1 garlic clove, chopped
- 1 lb. shelled fresh or thawed frozen fava beans
- large sprig of mint
- large sprig of chopped parsley
- 1 bay leaf
- salt and pepper

method

Cook the bacon in a heavy saucepan until the fat runs. Stir in the onion and garlic, and cook gently until they are softened.

Stir in the beans, herbs, and seasoning. Barely cover with water and simmer until the beans are tender, 6–15 minutes depending on the age of the beans; or cook according to the directions on the package if using frozen beans.

Strain and discard the bay leaf and mint. Serve immediately.

CHAPTER FIVE

Breads and Sauces

~

Firm crusty bread is an important part of the Portuguese diet. It is made in the traditional way, with unbleached strong flour, requiring plenty of kneading, long slow rising and brick ovens for baking. Rye flour and cornmeal are often included in the dough.
The Portuguese culinary repertoire does not include many sauces, but those that do exist are used frequently, such as Tomatada, Piri-piri and Refogado.

Piri-piri Sauce
Piri-piri

makes about 5 tablespoons

- ½ small red bell pepper, seeded, and sliced
- 4–5 fresh red chilis, seeded, and sliced
- juice of 1½ lemons
- 2 tsp. olive oil
- salt

This is a chili-based sauce that provides the fire in many savory dishes – it is easier to add a few drops of the ready-made chili-based sauce than to seed and chop chilis each time.

Like other traditional recipes, nearly everyone who makes Piri-piri has their own version, the simplest of which is to fill a third of a jar or bottle with small, hot red chilis, then top up with olive oil, cover and leave in a cool place for at least 1 month so the oil is impregnated with the heat of the chilis. Other versions, like the one below, include lemon juice or vinegar. Bottles of Piri-piri can also be bought. Hot pepper sauce can be substituted.

method

Simmer the red bell pepper and chilis in a saucepan with the lemon juice for about 15 minutes until tender.

Mix to a thick paste with the oil in a blender. Season with salt. Pour into a small bottle or jar, cover and keep in a cool place.

Onion Purée
Refogado

makes about 1 lb.

- 4 tsp. olive oil
- 18 oz. large onions, finely chopped
- salt and pepper
- 3 garlic cloves

This gently stewed mixture of onions and oil is the basis of many Portuguese dishes and sauces. It can be made in advance and stored for several days in the refrigerator.

method

Heat the oil in a heavy pan that has a lid. Stir in the onions, add salt, cover and cook over a very low heat for about 1 hour, until the onions have softened and almost disintegrated.

Add the garlic cloves, stir and increase the heat slightly. Leave to cook until the onions are an even brown. Remove the garlic, if preferred, and season to taste.

Clockwise from the top: Red Bell Pepper Paste, Tomato Sauce, Onion Purée, and Piri-piri Sauce.

Tomato Sauce
Tomatada

makes about 2½ cups

- 6 tbsp. olive oil
- 2 onions, chopped
- 1–2 garlic cloves, chopped
- 2 red bell peppers, cored, seeded, and sliced
- 1 fresh red chili, seeded and sliced
- 2¼ lb. well-flavored tomatoes, chopped
- salt and pepper

A tomato sauce is a staple for Portuguese cooks. The special taste is not only because their tomatoes are sweet and richly flavored, but because of the amount of oil that is used, so do not reduce the quantity; it emulsifies with the other ingredients when the sauce is boiled hard or puréed. Red bell peppers make this recipe even more special. For a greater depth of tomato flavor, add a few pieces of sun-dried tomatoes, or a little sun-dried tomato paste.

Tomato sauce is both used in recipes and served separately with eggs, meat, poultry, fish, and vegetables.

method

Heat the oil, add the onion and garlic and cook gently until beginning to soften. Stir in the bell peppers and chili, and cook for a few minutes; then add the tomatoes and simmer, stirring occasionally, until reduced to a sauce consistency.

Purée in a blender or food processor; then strain through a sieve to remove pieces of skin and the seeds. Season and reheat as required.

Migas
Migas

serves 4–5

- 14 oz. Pâo (see page 113)
- 1¼ cups boiling water
- 2 tbsp. olive oil
- 4 oz. piece bacon, cut into strips
- 1 onion, chopped
- 2 garlic cloves, chopped
- 4 tbsp. chopped cilantro
- salt and pepper

There is no easy, meaningful way to translate Migas – basically, it is made from bread that is fried, but to call the dish "Fried Bread" would be misleading. For Migas it is always essential to have good, firm bread, such as Pão (see page 113). There are a number of versions of the dish and in this one, which comes from Ribatejo, the bread – ideally containing a proportion of cornmeal – is softened in hot water before cooking; then, when cooked, it is rolled over in a similar way to an omelet. Serve with roast pork or fried eggs.

method

Crumble the bread, including the crust, into a bowl, add the water and leave to soak for 15 minutes. Mash with a fork.

Heat the oil in a non-stick skillet and fry the bacon until crisp and brown. Using a perforated spoon, add to the bread. Add the onion and garlic to the pan and fry until soft and golden. Using a perforated spoon, transfer to the bread mixture. Add the cilantro and seasoning, and mix together thoroughly.

Transfer the mixture to the pan and flatten it to make a cake. Fry for 10–15 minutes until the underside is becoming crusted and brown. Roll up the *migas* like an omelet; two spatulas will be a help – and don't worry if the *migas* breaks. Pat into a roll shape and continue to cook until brown and crusted underneath.

Red Bell Pepper Paste
Massa de pimentão

A paste of broiled red bell peppers has now become a fashionable ingredient, but it has been used in Portugal for many a long year as a flavoring for meat, poultry and fish, grills, and marinades. The garlic cloves can also be broiled, before peeling, if liked. The paste can be kept in a covered glass jar in the refrigerator for 2 weeks.

makes about 1 cup
- 3 large red bell peppers, seeded and quartered lengthwise
- 1 tbsp. sea salt
- 2 garlic cloves
- 4 tbsp. olive oil

method
Stir together the bell peppers and salt; then leave, uncovered, at room temperature for 24 hours.

Preheat the broiler. Rinse the bell peppers well, drain and pat dry. Place, skin side up, on a baking sheet. Broil until the skins are charred and blistered. Leave to cool slightly before peeling off the skins and discarding.

Purée the garlic and bell peppers in a blender, pouring in the oil slowly.

Country Bread
Pão

Portuguese bread is usually very good – firm, crusty and well-flavored. The best results can be obtained by using unbleached flour and baking the loaf on a preheated baking stone, which can be found in good cookware stores.

makes an 8 inch round loaf
- 1 lb. unbleached strong flour
- pinch of salt
- 2 tsp. active dry yeast
- 1 cup water
- olive oil

method
Stir the flour, salt, and yeast together in a mixing bowl. Make a well in the center and pour in the water slowly, stirring to draw in the dry ingredients to make a firm dough; add a little more water if necessary.

Form into a ball and transfer to a lightly floured surface. Knead well until smooth and elastic; this will take about 15 minutes. Form into a ball again.

Oil a bowl lightly, add the dough and turn to coat in the oil. Cover and leave to rise slowly in a draft-free place until doubled in volume.

Punch down the dough, turn on to a floured surface and knead again until smooth and elastic, about 5 minutes. Form into a ball about 8 inches in diameter, put on a lightly oiled baking sheet and leave to double in volume again.

Preheat the oven to 400°. Preheat a baking stone if using.

Transfer the loaf to the baking stone, if using. Bake for 15 minutes, then lower the oven temperature to 350° and bake for a further 15–20 minutes until well browned on top and the bottom sounds hollow when tapped. Cool on a wire rack.

Cornbread

Broa

makes I loaf

- 8 oz. fine cornmeal
- about 3 cups unbleached strong flour
- 2½ tsp. active dry yeast
- salt
- ¾ cup milk
- 1¼ cups water
- 1 tbsp. olive oil

This chewy bread comes from the Minho in northern Portugal. Sometimes barley and alfalfa flour are included. The bread is baked in flat rounds and usually accompanies soups.

method

Stir the cornmeal, flour, yeast, and salt together in a mixing bowl. Make a well in the center and pour in the milk and water gradually, mixing in the dry ingredients to make a soft but manageable dough.

Turn on to a floured work surface and knead for about 8–10 minutes, until firm and elastic. Form the dough into a ball. Oil a bowl, add the dough and turn to coat with the oil. Cover and leave in a draft-free place until doubled in volume.

Punch down the dough, turn it on to a floured surface and knead for a few minutes. Form into a round loaf and put on a lightly oiled baking sheet. Leave to double in volume again.

Preheat the oven to 350°. Bake the loaf for about 40 minutes or until the bottom sounds hollow when tapped.

Every two years in June and July, the people of Tomar celebrate the harvest in one of the most extraordinary festivals to be seen – the Festival of Tabuleiros.

CHAPTER SIX

Cakes
and Desserts

~

The Portuguese have a sweet
tooth fostered by, if not a direct
result of, the centuries of Moorish
occupation. The influence of the
Moors is evident in the many
sugar-laden almond confections,
sometimes flavoured with rose or
orange flower water. They are
also often egg-rich. Such
confections are available from
pastelerias (pastry shops) and
are enjoyed with a cup of tea or
coffee, as well as at the end of a
meal. There is excellent fruit in
Portugal, which many visitors
find to be the best dessert.

Egg Cakes in Syrup
Papos de anjo

serves 4–6
- butter
- 4 large egg yolks
- 1 large egg white
- 1 cup sugar
- ½ cup water
- few drops of vanilla or almond extract

The exact translation of the Portuguese title is "Angels' Breasts". It is another of the sweet, rich egg dishes so beloved by the Portuguese.

method

Preheat the oven to 350°. Butter 12 2 inch muffin pans, dariole molds or custard cups generously.

Whisk the egg yolks until very thick and pale. With a clean whisk, whisk the egg white until stiff but not dry; then stir 3 spoonfuls into the egg yolks. Fold in the remaining egg white gently. Divide between the pans or molds and stand in a roasting pan. Pour in sufficient boiling water to come halfway up the sides of the pans or dishes and bake for 15–20 minutes until set.

Meanwhile, heat the sugar in the water gently, stirring until dissolved; then boil until it is a thick syrup. Add a few drops of vanilla or almond extract.

Leave the cooked cakes to cool in the pans or dishes for a few minutes before unmolding. Dip them into the syrup and then put them into a large, shallow serving plate or bowl. Pour over the remaining syrup and chill well.

Caramel Custard
Pudim flan

serves 4
- 6 tbsp. sugar
- 4 tbsp. water
- 2 cups hot milk
- 3 eggs, separated
- 5 large egg yolks

Caramel custard is so widely and so frequently eaten in Portugal that it has been nicknamed "365", indicating the number of days in the year on which most restaurants serve it. Typically, Portuguese caramel custard is rich in egg yolks.

method

Preheat the oven to 350°. Place four dariole molds or custard cups in a baking pan.

Heat the sugar and water gently in a small heavy-based saucepan until the sugar has dissolved; then boil rapidly until golden brown. Remove from the heat and pour in the milk very slowly and carefully. Stir to dissolve the caramel completely. Beat the egg yolks lightly and stir in the caramel-flavored milk.

Strain the mixture into the molds and pour boiling water into the baking pan. Bake for 20–25 minutes until just set in the center. Remove the dishes from the baking pan and leave to cool. Cover and chill lightly.

Almond Tart
Torta de amêndoas

serves 6–8
- ½ cup cold unsalted butter, diced
- ½ cup superfine sugar
- 1 egg, beaten
- 1 cup all-purpose flour
- pinch of baking soda

topping
- ½ cup plus 2 tbsp. unsalted butter
- generous ½ cup superfine sugar
- generous 1 cup blanched almonds, slivered
- 3–4 tbsp. milk

Almonds were introduced into Portugal by the Moors. They are now grown in the Algarve, Alentejo and Madeira, and feature in many cakes, desserts, and sweetmeats. The sugar in this recipe has been reduced so it is less sweet than other Portuguese desserts, making it more acceptable to other palates. Although it is called a tart, it consists of a layer of a cake-type mixture which is then topped with an almond mixture.

method
Preheat the oven to 375°.

Cream the butter with the sugar; then gradually beat in the egg. Sift over the flour and baking soda and fold lightly into the butter mixture.

Turn into a buttered 8 inch loose-bottomed layer pan and bake for about 20–25 minutes until just springy to the touch in the center and lightly colored.

To make the topping, melt the butter gently in a heavy-based saucepan. Stir in the sugar, almonds, and milk, and heat without stirring, for 5–10 minutes, until lightly browned. Spread over the cake and bake for 10–12 minutes until golden. Leave to cool before serving.

Sweet Egg Cream
Ovos moles

serves 4–6
- generous ⅓ cup short-grain rice
- 2 cups water
- 1 cup sugar
- 8 large egg yolks

Ovos moles may be used as part of a number of Portuguese desserts and sweets, or may be served in small portions for a dessert. At Aveiro, on the Beira Litoral coast, it is traditionally sold in small wooden barrels or white shell-shaped containers. The use of the water from cooking rice is a fairly recent practice but it improves the texture of the cream. The cream can be kept for 2–3 weeks in a covered container in the refrigerator.

method
Simmer the rice in the water in a covered saucepan for about 30 minutes until tender. Strain and reserve ½ cup of the water. Discard the rice or use it for another dish.

Heat the sugar gently in the reserved rice water, stirring constantly, until the sugar has dissolved. Boil until reduced to a light syrup.

Cool slightly and then pour on to the egg yolks slowly, whisking. Pour back into the pan in which the syrup was made and heat very gently, stirring, until thickened; do not allow it to boil as it will curdle.

Use as required, or pour into a dish or individual dishes and leave to cool.

Baskets (ceira) for sale in a local market.

Sponge Cake
Pão-de-ló

Portuguese sponge cakes are usually deep golden yellow because they contain a high proportion of egg yolks, which are richly colored. Traditionally, more egg yolks than whites are used, which makes the cakes more dense than this version. Pão-de-ló can be topped, filled or served with Sweet Egg Cream (see page 120) and fruits (often soaked in wine or liqueurs), or used as the basis for a whole range of sweets, most often made and eaten at pastelerias (pastry or cake stores).

makes an 8 inch cake
- 8 large eggs, separated
- ½ cup superfine sugar
- ¾ cup all-purpose flour
- few drops of vanilla or almond extract (optional)

method
Preheat the oven to 350°.

Whisk the egg yolks with the sugar until thick and pale. Sift the flour over the surface in batches and fold in lightly, with the extract, if using, with a large metal spoon.

Using a clean whisk, whisk the egg whites until stiff. Stir 2 or 3 spoonfuls into the egg yolk mixture and fold in the remainder in three batches.

Turn into a non-stick 8 inch ring mold and bake for 15–20 minutes until springy to the touch and pale brown. Leave to cool for a few minutes before unmolding carefully on to a wire rack to cool completely.

This beautiful sand-colored facade is typical of those found in Lisbon.

Almond Paste Candies
Morgados

Almond paste is the starting-point for many Portuguese candies, which are a legacy of the Moorish occupation. Almond trees were introduced to Portugal by the Moors; the use of orange flower or rose water is also inherited from the Moors. For example, the paste may be colored and molded into shapes to resemble fruits, animals and so on, then put into small paper cases; it may be flavored with chocolate before shaping or coated in cocoa powder instead of being colored; it may be formed into balls and filled with Sweet Egg Cream (see page 120); or wrapped around white pumpkin candy. The freshness of the almonds is important.

makes 24
- 1 cup superfine sugar
- 4 tbsp. water
- 2 cups blanched almonds, ground
- few drops of orange flower or rose water or almond extract
- confectioners' sugar

method
Heat the sugar and water gently in a small saucepan until the sugar has dissolved; then boil to make a light syrup.

Add the almonds and stir over a low heat until very thick and dry. Mix in the orange flower or rose water or almond extract, turn on to a lightly oiled surface and leave to cool.

Sift a thin coating of confectioners' sugar over the work surface and form the almond paste into the required shapes. Leave to dry for a few days in a dry, airy place.

Sweet Milk Clouds
Doce de claras e ovos mole

This is a favorite dessert throughout Portugal, especially in restaurants.

method

Put the vanilla bean and milk in a heavy-based, preferably non-stick, saucepan and bring to a boil slowly. Remove from the heat, cover and leave for 20 minutes.

Whisk the egg yolks with ½ cup of the sugar until thick. Remove the vanilla bean from the milk and bring the milk back to a boil. Stir into the egg yolk mixture slowly and return to the pan. Heat very gently, stirring constantly, until thickened; do not allow it to boil.

Leave to cool, stirring occasionally, and then strain into a shallow serving bowl or individual bowls. Cover and chill.

Whisk the egg whites until stiff and whisk in the remaining sugar gradually.

Heat a wide, shallow pan of water to simmering point. Drop large spoonfuls of egg white on to the water, spacing them slightly apart, and poach gently for about 4 minutes, turning them after 2 minutes. Lift out with a perforated spoon and drain on several thicknesses of paper towels.

Float the "clouds" on the custard and serve.

serves 4
- 1 vanilla bean
- 2 cups milk
- 4 eggs, separated
- generous ½ cup sugar

Peaches in Red Wine
Pessago com vinho

During the peach-growing season, large bowls of these peaches are available at the Herdade de Zambujal, a huge peach-growing estate on the Costa Azul.

method

Preheat the oven to 350°.

Pour boiling water over the peaches and leave for about 30–60 seconds; then remove with a perforated spoon and slip off the skins. If the skins are stubborn, return the peaches briefly to the water.

Put the peaches into a baking dish which they just fit, tuck the cinnamon stick in between them and pour over enough wine to cover them. Sprinkle over the sugar and bake for 40–50 minutes until the peaches are tender.

Remove from the oven, discard the cinnamon stick, turn the peaches over and leave to cool in the wine, turning once or twice more.

Serve dusted lightly with ground cinnamon.

serves 6
- 6 peaches
- 1 cinnamon stick
- ½–¾ bottle of red wine
- ½ cup superfine sugar
- ground cinnamon, to serve

Rice Pudding
Arroz doce

serves 6
- about 7 cups milk
- 1 cinnamon stick
- 2–3 strips lemon peel
- ⅓ cup short-grain rice
- 5 tbsp. superfine sugar
- 3–4 egg yolks

A nationally favorite pudding, usually enriched with egg yolks and often flavored with lemon rind and cinnamon. The top is sometimes caramelized.

method
Reserve ½ cup of the milk. Bring the remaining milk, the cinnamon stick and lemon peel to a boil in a large saucepan. Stir in the rice, lower the heat so the water is barely simmering, and cook, stirring constantly, for 15 minutes.

Leave the rice to cook very gently for about 1 hour, stirring occasionally. Stir in the sugar and cook for about 45–55 minutes, stirring from time to time, until the milk has almost been absorbed.

Stir in the egg yolks and continue to cook very gently, stirring occasionally, until the pudding is very creamy and falls easily from the spoon; add some of the reserved milk if necessary.

Discard the cinnamon stick and lemon peel. Serve the rice pudding hot, or leave to cool and then chill lightly.

Sintra Cheesecakes
Queijadas de Sintra

makes 24
- 2–4 tbsp. butter or shortening, diced
- 2 cups all-purpose flour
- pinch of salt
- about ½ cup water

filling
- 1 cup superfine sugar
- ¼ cup ground almonds
- ½ tsp. ground cinnamon
- 1 cup fresh, soft sheep's cheese or ricotta or curd cheese, sieved
- 3 large egg yolks

Lord Byron so loved the interesting and captivating small town of Sintra, in the wooded hills above Estoril, that he called it an Eden on earth, and wrote part of "Childe Harold's Pilgrimage" there. Other people, such as the former Portuguese royal family, are also drawn to Sintra, with its collection of six architectural oddities, including a Moorish-style royal palace, and perhaps its small square cheesecakes, which are renowned. In Sintra, fresh, soft sheep's milk cheese is used, but ricotta or curd cheese will work well. The crisp, wafer-thin pastry is traditionally made with shortening, butter not being available; butter can be substituted but the pastry will not be as crisp.

method
To make the filling, stir together the sugar, ground almonds, and cinnamon; then beat into the cheese. Stir in the egg yolks over the surface first before folding in. Set aside.

Preheat the oven to 400°. Rub the fat into the flour and salt until the mixture resembles bread crumbs. Stir in enough water to make a dough that is not sticky. Transfer the dough to a lightly floured work surface, form into a ball and roll out as thinly as possible. Cut into 3½ inch circles with a lightly floured plain cutter or glass and use to line muffin pans. Half-fill with the cheese mixture. Bake the cheesecakes for about 15 minutes until just set in the center. Leave to cool slightly in the pans before removing to a wire rack to cool completely.

Honey and Orange Figs

Salada de laranjas

I almost invariably prefer fresh fruit, or a simple refreshing fruit dessert such as this one, to the somewhat too sweet Portuguese desserts.

method

Stir the honey into the fruit juices until it has dissolved. Put the fruit into a dish, pour over the honey mixture and stir together lightly. Cover and chill for at least 1 hour.

Stir gently before dividing between 4 chilled dishes. Decorate each serving with a sprig of mint.

serves 4

- 2 tbsp. clear honey
- 1 tbsp. lemon juice
- 4 tbsp. orange juice
- 4 ripe figs, sliced into rings
- 2 oranges, peeled and segmented
- 4 mint sprigs

Apricot Tart
Torta de alperche

All the elements of this tart complement each other perfectly – the lush, soft filling, topped by juicy, sweet apricots held in an almond-flavored pastry. The best cheese to use is ricotta, or failing that, medium- or full-fat curd cheese.

method

Stir the flour, sugar, half the orange peel and a pinch of sugar together in a bowl. Make a well in the center and add the egg yolk, vanilla extract, and butter. Using your fingertips, mix together to make a smooth dough, adding 1–2 tsp. orange juice. Cover and chill.

Preheat the oven to 400°. Roll out half the dough and use to line the bottom of a buttered 9 inch loose-bottomed, spring-form cake pan. Bake for 15 minutes and then leave to cool.

Meanwhile, make the filling. Beat the cheese with the sugar and remaining orange peel; then gradually beat in the eggs. Stir in the cream and almond extract.

Roll out the remaining pastry and use to line the sides of the cake pan, pressing the bottom edge on to the partly cooked base. Pour in the filling and bake for 15 minutes; then lower the temperature to 325° and bake for 20 minutes until just set.

Plunge the apricots into boiling water, leave for a few seconds, then lift out and remove the skin. Halve the fruit and remove the pits. Arrange the apricots over the filling and bake for 10 minutes.

Leave to cool in the pan before transferring to a serving dish. Heat apricot jam and remaining orange juice. Brush over the apricots.

serves 6–8
- 1¼ cups all-purpose flour
- 5 tbsp. superfine sugar
- finely grated peel and juice of 1 orange
- 1 egg yolk
- ¼ tsp. vanilla extract
- ½ cup plus 2 tbsp. unsalted butter, diced

filling
- 1 lb. ricotta or curd cheese
- 1 cup superfine sugar
- 4 eggs
- 6 tbsp. heavy cream
- few drops of almond extract

topping
- 1 lb. apricots
- 2 tbsp. apricot jam

Nun's Belly
Barriga de freira

In Portugal, as in many other countries, nuns made and often sold sweetmeats, cakes, cookies, and preserves.

method

Heat the sugar in the water gently, stirring occasionally, until the sugar has dissolved; then boil to a fairly thick syrup. Remove from the heat, stir in the butter until it has melted and then mix in the bread crumbs. Put the saucepan over a very low heat and stir in the egg yolks gradually. Cook, stirring constantly, until thickened; do not allow the mixture to boil. Transfer to a serving dish and sprinkle with ground cinnamon and toasted almonds.

serves 4
- 1 cup sugar
- ¾ cup water
- 2 tbsp. unsalted butter, diced
- 4 cups fresh white bread crumbs
- 8 egg yolks, beaten
- ground cinnamon and toasted slivered almonds for decoration

Apricot Tart

Index

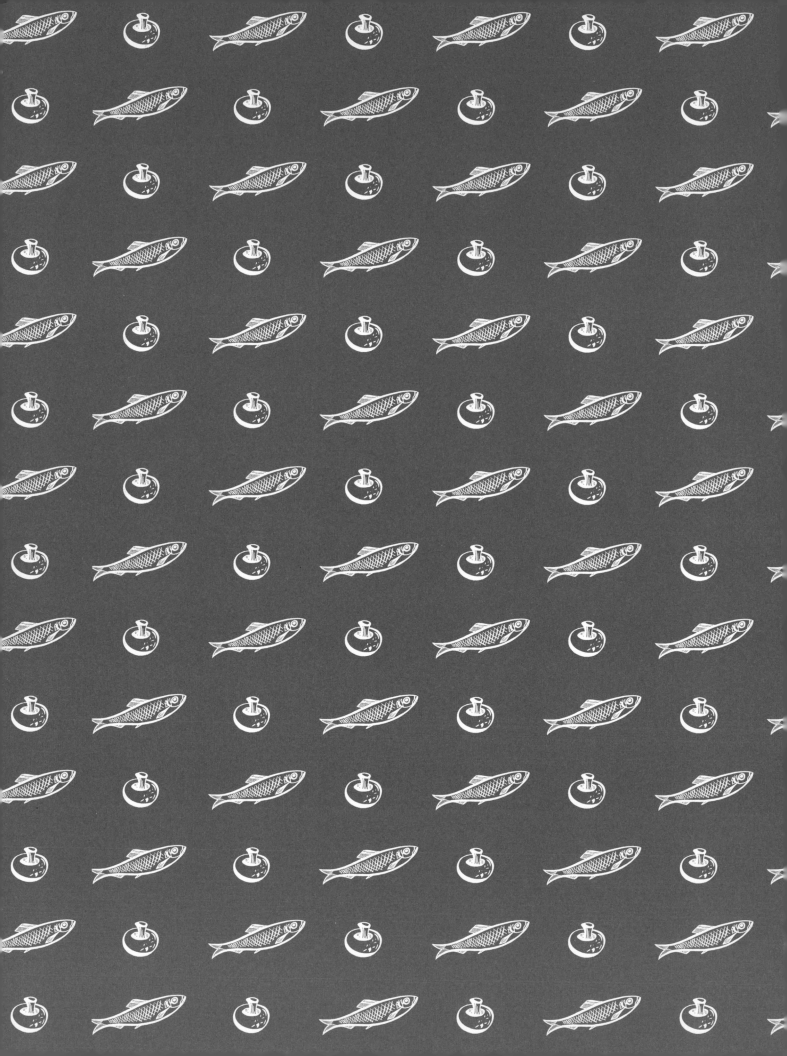